D.

FANTASTIC BEASTS

AND WHERE TO FIND THEM™

The
Original Screenplay

Also By J. K. Rowling
From Clipper Large Print

Harry Potter and the Cursed Child –
Parts One and Two (Dyslexia Edition)

J.K. ROWLING

FANTASTIC BEASTS

AND WHERE TO FIND THEM

W F HOWES LTD

This large print edition published in 2016 by
W F Howes Ltd
Unit 5, St George's House, Rearsby Business Park,
Gaddesby Lane, Rearsby, Leicester LE7 4YH

1 3 5 7 9 10 8 6 4 2

First published in the United Kingdom in 2016
by Little, Brown

A CIP catalogue record for this book is available
from the British Library

ISBN 978 1 51005 458 5

Typeset by Palimpsest Book Production Limited,
Falkirk, Stirlingshire

Printed and bound by Printforce Nederland b.v.

**To the memory
of Gordon Murray,
real-life creature-healer
and hero**

Contents

Scene 1

Ext. Somewhere in Europe—1926—Night

A large, isolated, derelict chateau emerges from the darkness. We focus on a cobbled square outside the building shrouded in mist, eerie, silent.

Five Aurors stand, wands aloft, tentative as they edge towards the chateau. A sudden explosion of pure white light sends them flying.

We whip round to find their bodies scattered, lying motionless at the entrance to a large parkland. A figure (Grindelwald) enters the frame, his back to the camera; ignoring the bodies, he stares out

into the night sky, as we pan up towards the moon.

Montage: we see various magical newspaper headlines from 1926 relating to Grindelwald's attacks all over the world – 'Grindelwald Strikes Again In Europe', 'Hogwarts School Increases Security', 'Where is Grindelwald?'. He's a serious threat to the magical community and he's vanished. Moving photos detail destroyed buildings, fires, screaming victims. The articles come thick and fast – the worldwide hunt for Grindelwald continues. We push in on a final article displaying the Statue of Liberty.

Transition to:

Scene 2

Ext. Ship Gliding into New York—Next Morning

A bright, clear New York day. Seagulls swoop overhead.

A large passenger ship glides past the Statue of Liberty. Passengers lean over the rails, looking excitedly towards the oncoming land.

Push in towards a figure sitting on a bench with his back to us – Newt Scamander, weatherbeaten, wiry, wearing an old blue overcoat. Beside him rests a battered brown leather case. A catch on the case flicks open of its own accord. Newt swiftly bends down to close it.

Placing the case on his lap, Newt leans in, whispering.

Newt
   Dougal – you settle down now, please. It won't be long.

Scene 3

Ext. New York—Day

Aerial Shot of New York.

Scene 4

Ext. Ship/Int. Customs—Shortly Afterwards—Day

Among bustling crowds, Newt walks down the gangplank of the ship, as we push in towards his case.

Customs Official **(O.S.)**
Next.

Newt stands at the Customs – a long row of desks by the shipyard, manned by serious-looking American officials. A Customs Official examines Newt's very tattered British passport.

Customs Official
British, huh?

Newt
   Yes.

Customs Official
   First trip to New York?

Newt
   Yes.

Customs Official **(gesturing to Newt's case)**
   Anything edible in there?

Newt **(placing a hand over his breast pocket)**
   No.

Customs Official
   Livestock?

The catch on Newt's case flicks open again. Newt looks down and hastily closes it.

Newt
   Must get that fixed – ah, no.

Customs Official **(suspicious)**
   Let me take a look.

Newt places the case on the desk between them and discreetly flicks a brass dial to 'Muggleworthy'.

The Customs Official spins the case towards him and pops the catches, lifting the lid to reveal pyjamas, various maps, a journal, an alarm clock, a magnifying glass and a Hufflepuff scarf. Finally satisfied, he closes the case.

Customs Official
   Welcome to New York.

Newt
   Thank you.

Newt gathers his passport and case.

Customs Official
   Next!

Newt exits through Customs.

Scene 5

Ext. Street near City Hall Subway—Dusk

A long street of identical brown-stone houses, one of which has been reduced to rubble. A gaggle of reporters and photographers mills around in the vague hope of something happening, but without much enthusiasm. One Reporter is interviewing an excitable middle-aged man as they move through the rubble.

Witness
    —and it was like a – like a **wind** or like a – like a **ghost** – but dark – and I saw its eyes – shinin' white eyes—

Reporter (expressionless – notebook in his hand)
 —a dark wind – with eyes ...

Witness
 —like a dark **mass**, and it dove down there, down underground – I swear to God ... into the earth right in front of me.

Close on Percival Graves as he walks towards the destroyed building.

Graves: smart clothing, very handsome, early middle-age, his demeanour differs from those around him. He is watchful, tightly coiled, an air of intense confidence.

Photographer (sotto voce)
 Hey – did you get anything?

Reporter (sotto voce)
 Dark wind, blah blah.

Photographer
 It's some atmospheric hooey. Or electrical.

Graves moves up the steps of the now-ruined building. He examines the destruction, curious, alert.

Reporter
Hey – you thirsty?

Photographer
Nah, I'm on the wagon. Promised Martha I'd lay off.

The wind begins to pick up, swirling around the building, accompanied by a high-pitched screeching. Graves alone looks interested.

A sudden series of bangs at street level. All turn to look for the source of the sound: a wall cracks, the rubble on the floor begins to shake before exploding like an earthquake, ripping out of the building and down through the middle of the street. The movement is violent, rushed – people and cars go flying.

The mysterious force then flies up into the air, swirling through the city,

diving in and out of alleyways, before crashing down into a subway station.

Close on Graves, as he examines the destruction of the street.

A mingled roar and howl emanates from the bowels of the earth.

Scene 6

Ext. New York Street— Day

Watching Newt walk, we see in him an unselfconscious Keatonesque quality, a sense of a different rhythm to those around him. In his hand he clutches directions on a small piece of paper, but he still shows a scientist's curiosity about this alien environment.

Scene 7

Ext. Another Street, Steps of the City Bank—Day

Newt, intrigued by the noise of shouting, approaches a rally of the New Salem Philanthropic Society.

Mary Lou Barebone, a handsome mid-western woman in a 1920s version of Puritan dress, charismatic and earnest, stands on a small stage at the steps to the City Bank. Behind her stands a man parading a banner emblazoned with the organisation's symbol: hands proudly grasping a broken wand amid bright yellow and red flames.

Mary Lou **(to the assembled crowd)**
... this great city sparkles with the jewels of man's invention! Movie theatres, automobiles, the wireless, electric lights – all dazzle and bewitch us!

Newt slows down and watches Mary Lou as he would observe a foreign species: no judgement, simply interest. Nearby stands Tina Goldstein, hat low on her head, upturned collar. She is eating a hot dog, mustard smeared on her upper lip. Newt accidently bumps into her as he makes his way to the front of the rally.

Newt
Oh ... so sorry.

Mary Lou
But where there is light there is shadow, friend.
Something is stalking our city, wreaking destruction and then disappearing without a trace ...

Jacob Kowalski moves nervously down the street towards the crowd,

wearing an ill-fitting suit and carrying a battered brown leather case.

Mary Lou **(O.S.)**
We have to fight – join us, the Second Salemers, in our fight!

Jacob makes his way through the gathered crowd, also pushing past Tina.

Jacob
Excuse me doll, just trying to get to the bank – excuse me – just trying ...

Jacob trips over Newt's case, disappearing momentarily. Newt hauls him up.

Newt
I'm so sorry – my case—

Jacob
No harm done—

Jacob struggles on, heading past Mary Lou and up the steps of the bank.

Jacob
Excuse me!

The kerfuffle around Newt draws Mary Lou's attention.

Mary Lou **(charming, to Newt)**
You, friend! What drew you to our meeting today?

Newt is startled to find himself the centre of attention.

Newt
Oh ... I was just ... passing ...

Mary Lou
Are you a seeker? A seeker after truth?

A beat.

Newt
I'm more of a chaser, really.

Angle on people moving in and out of the bank.

A smartly dressed man flips a dime towards a beggar sitting on the steps.

Close **On the dime, falling in slow motion.**

Mary Lou **(O.S.)**
Hear my words and heed my warning ...

Angle **on** **some little paws, which have appeared in the narrow crack between the lid and the body of Newt's case.**

Angle **on** **the dime hitting the steps with a musical clang.**

Angle **on** **the paws, now trying hard to prise open the case.**

Mary Lou
... and laugh if you dare: **witches live among us!**

Mary Lou's three adopted children, adults Credence and Chastity, and Modesty (an eight-year-old girl), hand out leaflets. Credence appears nervous and troubled.

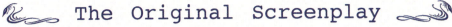

Mary Lou **(O.S.)**
We have to fight together for the sake of our children – for the sake of tomorrow!

(to Newt)

What do you say to that, friend?

As Newt looks up towards Mary Lou, something seen from the corner of his eye catches his attention. The Niffler, a small furry black cross between a mole and a duck-billed platypus, is sitting on the steps of the bank, hastily pulling the beggar's hat full of money out of sight behind a pillar.

Newt, startled, looks down at his case.

Angle on the Niffler, busy shovelling the beggar's coins into a pouch in its belly. The Niffler looks up, notices Newt's gaze, and hurriedly gathers the rest of the coins before tumbling away and into the bank.

Newt jolts forwards.

Newt
Excuse me.

Angle on Mary Lou – she looks confused at Newt's lack of interest in her cause.

Mary Lou **(O.S.)**
Witches live among us.

Angle on Tina, moving through the crowd, eyeing Newt suspiciously.

Scene 8

Int. Lobby of Bank—
Moments Later—Day

A large, impressive-looking bank atrium. In the centre, behind a golden counter, clerks are busy at work serving customers.

Newt skids to a halt in the entrance of the space and looks around for his creature. His dress and demeanour make him out of place among the smartly dressed New Yorkers.

Bank Employee **(suspicious)**
    Can I help you, sir?

Newt
    No, I was just ... just ... waiting ...

Newt motions towards a bench and backs away, taking a seat next to Jacob.

Tina peers at Newt from behind a pillar.

Jacob **(nervous)**
  Hi. What brings you here?

Newt is desperately trying to spot his Niffler.

Newt
  Same as you ...

Jacob
  You're here to get a loan to open up a bakery?

Newt **(looking around – preoccupied)**
  Yes.

Jacob
  What are the odds of that? Well, may the best man win, I guess.

Newt spots the Niffler, which is now stealing coins from someone's bag.

Jacob holds out his hand, but Newt is off.

Newt
Excuse me.

Newt darts away. In his place on the bench lies a large silver egg.

Jacob
Hey, mister ... hey mister!

Newt doesn't hear; he is too engaged in hunting the Niffler.

Jacob picks up the egg just as the door into the Bank Manager's office opens, and a Secretary looks out.

Jacob
Hey, fella!

Secretary
Mr Kowalski, Mr Bingley will see you now.

Pocketing the egg, Jacob heads towards the office, steeling himself.

Jacob **(sotto voce)**
Okay ... okay.

Angle on Newt, surreptitiously pursuing the Niffler as it moves through the bank. He finally spots it removing a glittering buckle from a lady's shoe before scurrying onwards, eager for more shiny objects.

As Newt watches, helpless, the Niffler jumps lithely between cases and into bags, snatching and pilfering.

Scene 9

Int. Bingley's Office—Moments Later—Day

Jacob is facing the imposing and impeccably suited Mr Bingley. Bingley is examining Jacob's business proposal for a bakery.

An uncomfortable silence. The sound of a ticking clock and Bingley murmuring.

Jacob looks down at his pocket – the egg has started to vibrate.

Bingley
You are currently working ... in a canning factory?

Jacob

That's the best I can do – I only got back in '24.

Bingley

Got back?

Jacob

From Europe, sir. Yeah – I was part of the Expeditionary Forces there—

Jacob is clearly nervous, miming a digging action to the words 'Expeditionary Forces', in the vain hope that a joke might help his cause.

Scene 10

Int. Back Room of the Bank—Moments Later—Day

We cut back to Newt in the bank – in seeking the Niffler he has ended up waiting in line for a bank teller. He cranes his neck, peering towards the bag of a lady at the front of the line. Tina watches him from behind a pillar.

Angle on coins spilling from underneath a bench.

Angle on Newt, who hears the coins and turns to see small paws hastily gathering them up.

Angle on the Niffler sitting under the bench looking fat and smug. Not yet satisfied, its

attention is caught by the shiny
tag hanging around the neck of
a small dog. The Niffler moves
slowly, cheekily, forwards – little
paw outstretched to grab the tag.
The dog snarls and barks.

Newt starts forwards and dives
under the bench – the Niffler runs,
scuttling over the bank counter
screens and out of Newt's reach.

Scene 11

Int. Bingley's Office—Moments Later—Day

Jacob opens his case with great pride. Inside is displayed a selection of his home-made pastries.

Jacob **(O.S.)**
　All right.

Bingley
　Mr Kowalski—

Jacob
　—you gotta try the paczki okay, it's my grandmother's recipe, the orange zest – just—

**Jacob holds out a paczki ...
Bingley is not distracted.**

Bingley
> Mr Kowalski, what do you propose to offer the bank as collateral?

Jacob
> Collateral?

Bingley
> Collateral.

Jacob gestures hopefully towards his pastries.

Bingley
> There are machines now that can produce hundreds of doughnuts an hour—

Jacob
> I know, I know, but they're nothing like what I can do—

Bingley
> The bank must be protected, Mr Kowalski. Good day to you.

Bingley dismissively rings a bell on his desk.

Scene 12

Int. Behind the Bank Counters—Moments Later—Day

The Niffler sits on a trolley covered in money bags, which it greedily empties into its pouch. As Newt watches through the security bars, aghast, a guard pushes the trolley away down a corridor.

Scene 13

Int. Bank, Hall—
Moments Later—Day

Jacob, downcast, exits Bingley's office. His bulging pocket vibrates. Alarmed, he pulls out the egg and looks around.

Angle on the Niffler, still sitting on the trolley, which is now being pushed into an elevator.

Angle on Jacob, who sees Newt in the distance.

Jacob
     Hey, Mr English guy! I think your egg is hatching.

Newt looks hurriedly between Jacob

and the shutting elevator doors
before making a decision: he points
his wand at Jacob. Jacob and the
egg are pulled magically across the
bank atrium towards Newt. In a split
second, they Disapparate.

Tina stares, incredulous, from
behind a pillar.

Scene 14

Int. Back Room of the Bank/Staircase—Day

Newt and Jacob Apparate into a narrow stairwell leading to the bank's vaults, suddenly past the tellers and security guards.

Newt gently takes the egg back from Jacob as it hatches, revealing a small blue, snake-like bird – an Occamy. Newt, his face full of wonder, looks to Jacob as though expecting a similar reaction from him.

Slowly, Newt carries the baby creature down the stairs.

Jacob

Excuse me ...

Jacob, very confused, looks back up the stairs towards the main bank atrium. On seeing Bingley approaching, he ducks down the stairs, out of sight.

Jacob

(to himself)

I was – over there. I was – over there?

Scene 15

Int. Basement Corridor of Bank Leading to Vault—Day

Jacob's POV: Newt is crouched down, opening his case. He carefully places the hatched Occamy inside, whispering tenderly:

Newt
  In you hop ...

Jacob **(O.S.)**
  Hello?

Newt
  No. Everyone settle down – stay.
Dougal, don't make me come in
there ...

Jacob moves along the corridor, staring at Newt.

We see a strange green crea- ture, part stick insect, part plant, poke its head out of Newt's breast pocket, intrigued. This is Pickett, a Bowtruckle.

Newt
Don't make me come down there.

Newt looks up to see the Niffler squeezing itself through locked doors, into the central vault.

Newt
Absolutely not!

Newt takes out his wand and points it at the vault.

Newt
Alohomora.

We watch the locks and cogs of the vault door turn.

Bingley comes round the corner, just as the vault door starts to open.

Bingley **(to Jacob)**
Oh, so you're gonna **steal** the money, huh?

Bingley hits a button on the wall. An alarm sounds. Newt aims his wand ...

Newt
Petrificus Totalus.

Bingley suddenly stiffens and falls back flat on the ground. Jacob cannot believe his eyes.

Jacob
Mr Bingley!

The vault door opens wide.

Mr Bingley **(in his paralysed state)**
... Kowalski!

Newt hurries into the vault. Inside he finds the Niffler lying among hundreds of opened deposit boxes,

and seated on a great pile of cash.
The Niffler stares at Newt defiantly
as it forces another gold bar into its
already overflowing pouch.

Newt
　　Really?!

Newt grasps the Niffler tightly and
turns it upside down, shaking it by
its hind legs. An extraordinary, and
seemingly endless, number of precious
items fall out.

Newt
　　(to the Niffler)

No ...

Jacob looks around him in
disbelief, an almost queasy fear.

Despite their altercation, Newt is
fond of the Niffler. He grins as he
tickles its stomach, causing more
treasure to pour out.

Footsteps on the stairs as several armed guards run down and into the vault corridor.

Jacob
(panicking)

Oh no ... no ... don't shoot. Don't shoot!

Newt quickly seizes Jacob and the two of them, plus the Niffler and case, Disapparate.

Scene 16

Ext. Deserted Side Street Next to the Bank—Day

Newt and Jacob Apparate into a side street. Security alarms ring out from the bank and, at the end of the side street, we see crowds gathering, police arriving.

Tina runs out of the bank and looks down. She sees Newt wrestling the Niffler back into the case, Jacob cowering by a wall.

Jacob
Ahhh!

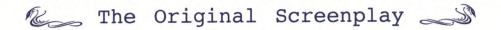

Newt
    For the last time, you pilfering pest –
paws off what doesn't belong to you!

**Newt shuts his case, then looks
around at Jacob.**

Newt
    I'm awfully sorry about all that—

Jacob
    What the **hell** was that?

Newt
    Nothing that need concern you. Now
unfortunately you have seen far too
much, so if you wouldn't mind – if you
just stand there – this will be over in
a jiffy.

**Newt, trying to find his wand,
turns his back on Jacob. Jacob takes
the opportunity, seizes his case, and
swings it violently at Newt, who is
knocked to the ground.**

Jacob
    Sorry—

Jacob runs for his life.

Newt holds his head for a moment and looks after Jacob, who has hurried down the alleyway and into the crowd.

Newt
   Bugger!

Tina comes walking down the side street with purpose. Newt gathers himself, picks up the case and, trying to be nonchalant, walks towards her. As he passes her, Tina grabs Newt's elbow and they Disapparate.

Scene 17

Ext. Narrow Alleyway Opposite Bank—Day

Newt and Tina Apparate into a cramped, bricked-up alleyway. We can still hear police sirens sounding in the background.

Tina, incredulous and out of breath, rounds on Newt.

Tina
  Who **are** you?

Newt
  I'm sorry?

Tina
  Who **are you**?

Newt

    Newt Scamander. And you are?

Tina

    What's that **thing** in your case?

Newt

    That's my Niffler.

(pointing at hot dog mustard still on Tina's lip)

    Er, you've got something on your—

Tina

    Why in the name of Deliverance Dane did you let that thing loose?

Newt

    I didn't mean to – he's incorrigible, you see, anything shiny, he's all over the place—

Tina

    You didn't mean to?

Newt

    No.

Tina
   You could not have chosen a worse
time to let that creature loose! We're
in the middle of a situation here! I'm
taking you in.

Newt
   You're taking me where?

**She produces her official ID card.
It bears her moving picture and an
impressive symbol of an American
eagle: Macusa.**

Tina
   Magical Congress of the United States
of America.

Newt **(nervous)**
   So, you work for **Macusa**? What are
you, some kind of investigator?

Tina **(hesitates)**
   Uh huh.

**She stuffs her identification card
back into her coat.**

Tina
Can you please tell me you took care of the No-Maj?

Newt
The what?

Tina (becoming irritated)
The No-Maj! No-magic – the non-wizard!

Newt
Oh sorry, we call them Muggles.

Tina (getting really worried)
You wiped his memory, right? The No-Maj with the case?

Newt
Um ...

Tina (appalled)
That's a Section 3A, Mr Scamander. I'm taking you in.

She takes Newt by the arm and they Disapparate again.

Scene 18

Ext. Broadway—Day

An ornately carved, incredibly tall skyscraper on the corner of a bustling street – the Woolworth Building.

Newt and Tina hurry along Broadway towards this building, Tina almost dragging Newt by his coat sleeve.

Tina
    Come on.

Newt
    Er – sorry but I do have things to do, actually.

Tina
> Well, you'll have to rearrange them!

Tina forcefully guides Newt through the busy traffic.

Tina
> What are you doing in New York anyway?

Newt
> I came to buy a birthday present.

Tina
> Couldn't you have done that in London?

They have arrived outside the Woolworth Building. Workers move in and out of a large revolving door.

Newt
> No, there's only one breeder of Appaloosa Puffskeins in the world and he lives in New York, so no ...

Tina moves Newt towards a side door, guarded by a man in a cloaked uniform.

Tina (to the guard)
I got a Section 3A.

The guard immediately opens the door.

Scene 19

Int. Woolworth Building Reception—Day

A normal 1920s office atrium, people milling around and chatting.

Tina **(O.S.)**
Hey. By the way, we closed that guy down a year ago. We don't allow the breeding of magical creatures in New York.

Pan around to watch Tina come through the door with Newt. As they enter, the whole entrance magically transforms from the Woolworth Building to the Magical Congress of the United States of America (Macusa).

Scene 20

Int. Macusa Lobby—Day

Newt's POV, as they move up a wide staircase and enter the main lobby – a vast, impressive space with impossibly high vaulted ceilings.

High up, a gigantic dial with many cogs and faces emblazoned with the legend: Magical Exposure Threat Level. The hand on the dial points to Severe: Unexplained Activity. Behind hangs an imposing portrait of a majestic-looking witch: Seraphina Picquery, Macusa's President.

Owls circulate, witches and wizards in 1920s dress are hard at work.

**Tina guides an impressed-looking
Newt through the bustle. They pass
several wizards sitting in a line,
waiting to have their wands shined
by a house-elf who operates a
complex contraption of feathers.**

**Newt and Tina reach an elevator.
The doors open to reveal Red,
a goblin bellboy.**

Red
Hey, Goldstein.

Tina
Hey, Red.

Tina pushes Newt inside.

Scene 21

Int. Elevator Day

Tina **(to Red)**
Major Investigation Department.

Red
I thought you was—

Tina
Major Investigation Department!
I got a Section 3A!

Red uses a long clawed stick to reach an elevator button above his head. The elevator descends.

Scene 22

Int. Major Investigation Department—Day

Close on a newspaper – The New York Ghost – **with the headline 'Magical Disturbances Risk Wizarding Exposure'.**

A group of the highest-level Aurors in the organisation are gathered together in serious discussion. Among them are Graves, examining the newspaper, his face cut and bruised from last night's encounter with the strange entity, and Madam Picquery herself.

Madam Picquery
The International Confederation is threatening to send a delegation. They think this is related to Grindelwald's attacks in Europe.

Graves
I was there. This is a beast. No human could do what this thing is capable of, Madam President.

Madam Picquery (O.S.)
Whatever it is, one thing's clear – it must be stopped. It's terrorising No-Majs, and when No-Majs are afraid, they attack. This could mean exposure. It could mean war.

On hearing footsteps, the group looks round to see Tina, who approaches cautiously, leading Newt.

Madam Picquery (angry but contained)
I made your position here quite clear, Miss Goldstein.

Tina (frightened)
Yes, Madam President, but I—

Madam Picquery
You are no longer an Auror.

Tina
No, Madam President, but—

Madam Picquery
Goldstein.

Tina
There's been a minor incident—

Madam Picquery
Well, this office is currently concerned with very major incidents. Get out.

Tina (humiliated)
Yes, ma'am.

Tina pushes a bemused-looking Newt back towards the elevator. Graves looks after them, the only one to appear sympathetic.

Scene 23

Int. Basement—Day

The elevator descends rapidly
through the long shaft.

The doors open onto a cramped,
airless, windowless basement
room. A painful contrast to the
floor above. Clearly the place
where utter no-hopers work.

Tina leads Newt past a hundred
typewriters clacking away
unmanned, with a tangle of glass
pipes hanging down from the
ceiling above them.

As each memo or form is
completed by a typewriter,
it folds itself into an origami rat,

which scurries up the appropriate
tube to the offices above. Two
rats collide and fight, tearing each
other apart.

Tina walks towards a dingy
corner of the room.
A sign: Wand Permit Office.

Newt ducks under it.

Scene 24

Int. Wand Permit Office—Day

The Wand Permit Office is only slightly larger than a cupboard. There are piles of unopened wand applications.

Tina stops behind a desk, removing her coat and hat. She tries to regain her lost status in front of Newt by appearing official, busying herself with papers.

Tina
So, you got your wand permit? All foreigners have to have them in New York.

Newt (lying)
I made a postal application weeks ago.

Tina (now sitting on the desk, scribbles on a clipboard)
Scamander ...

(finding him very fishy)

And you were just in Equatorial Guinea?

Newt
I've just completed a year in the field. I'm writing a book about magical creatures.

Tina
Like – an extermination guide?

Newt
No. A guide to help people understand why we should be protecting these creatures instead of killing them.

Abernathy (O.S.)
Goldstein! Where is she? Where is she? **Goldstein**!

Tina ducks behind her desk, which amuses Newt.

Abernathy, a pompous jobsworth, enters. He immediately realises where Tina is hidden.

Abernathy
  Goldstein!

Tina, looking guilty, slowly emerges from behind the desk.

Abernathy
  Did you just butt in on the Investigative Team again?

Tina is about to defend herself, but Abernathy continues.

Abernathy
  Where've you been?

Tina **(awkward)**
  What ...?

Abernathy **(to Newt)**
  Where'd she pick you up?

Newt
> Me?

**Newt quickly looks at Tina,
who shakes her head, her expression
one of desperation. Newt stalls –
a silent pact between him and Tina.**

Abernathy **(agitated by the lack of
information)**
> Have you been tracking them Second
> Salemers again?

Tina
> Of course not, sir.

**Graves comes round the corner.
Abernathy is immediately cowed.**

Abernathy
> Afternoon, Mr Graves, sir!

Graves
> Afternoon, ah – Abernathy.

**Tina steps forwards to formally
address Graves.**

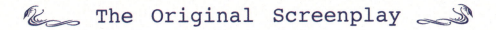

Tina
   **(speaking quickly, eager to have
her case heard)**

   Mr Graves, sir, this is Mr
Scamander – he has a crazy creature
in that case and it got out and caused
mayhem in a bank, sir.

Graves
   Let's see the little guy.

   **Tina breathes a sigh of relief:
finally someone is listening to her.
Newt tries to speak up – he looks
more panicky than might seem
warranted by a Niffler – but Graves
dismisses him.**

   **Tina theatrically places the case
onto a table and throws open the lid.
She looks aghast at the contents.**

   **Angle on the case contents – it
is full of pastries. Newt approaches,
nervous. On seeing the contents
he looks horrified. Graves looks
confused, but smirks slightly –
another one of Tina's mistakes.**

Graves
> Tina ...

Graves walks away. Newt and Tina stare at each other.

Scene 25

Ext. Street on the Lower East Side—Day

Jacob marches along the overcast street, case in hand, past pushcarts, shabby little shops and tenement buildings. He continually throws nervous glances over his shoulder.

Scene 26

Int. Jacob's Room—Day

A tiny, dirty room, the furnishings sparse and shabby.

Close on the case as Jacob throws it down onto his bed. He looks up at a portrait of his grandmother, which hangs on the wall.

Jacob
I'm sorry, Grandma.

Jacob sits down at his desk, hanging his head in his hands, downcast, tired. Behind him, one of the catches on the case flies open. Jacob turns ...

He sits down on the bed and examines the case. The second catch now flicks open of its own accord, and the case begins to shake, emitting aggressive animalistic sounds. Jacob slowly backs away.

Tentatively, he leans forward ... suddenly the lid flies open and out bursts a Murtlap – a rat-like creature with an anemone-style growth on its back. Jacob grapples with it, holding it tightly in both hands as it struggles.

We whip back to the case, which flies open once again as an invisible being shoots out, crashing into the ceiling before smashing through the window.

The Murtlap lunges forwards, biting Jacob on the neck, sending him crashing through furniture and tumbling to the ground.

The room shakes heavily, and the wall holding the picture of Jacob's grandma begins to crack before exploding, as more creatures escape off-screen.

Scene 27

Int. Second Salem Church, Main Hall— Day—Montage

A dingy wooden church with darkened windows and a high mezzanine balcony. Modesty is playing a solitary variation of hopscotch, skipping in and out of a chalked grid.

Modesty
  My momma, your momma, gonna catch a witch

  My momma, your momma, flying on a switch

  My momma, your momma, witches never cry

  My momma, your momma, witches gonna die!

As she sings we see the church is full of group paraphernalia – leaflets advertising Mary Lou's campaign, and a large version of the group's anti-witchcraft banner.

Scene 28

Int. Second Salem Church, Main Hall—Day

A pigeon coos from a high-up window. Credence steps forwards, staring up towards it before mechanically clapping his hands. The pigeon flies away.

We follow Chastity as she moves through the church and opens the large double doors onto the street.

Scene 29

Ext. Second Salem
Church, Backyard—Day

**Chastity emerges from
the church and rings a large
dinner bell.**

Scene 30

Int. Second Salem Church, Main Hall—Day

Modesty continues playing hopscotch. Credence pauses, looking past her and out towards the door.

Modesty
  Witch number three,
gonna watch her burn,

  Witch number four,
flogging take a turn.

  Young children stream into the church.

  Time Cut:

Brown soup is being ladled out to

the children, who jostle each other to get near the front of the line. Mary Lou, wearing an apron and looking on approvingly, squeezes through the little crowd.

Mary Lou
    Collect your leaflets before you get food, children.

Several of the children turn towards Chastity, who waits primly, handing out campaign leaflets.

Time Cut:

Mary Lou and Credence ladle out soup, Credence looking intently into every face.

A Boy with a birthmark on his face reaches the front of the line. Credence stops his work and stares at him. Mary Lou reaches out to touch the Boy's face.

Boy
    Is it a witch's mark, ma'am?

Mary Lou
  No. He's okay.

**The Boy takes his soup and leaves.
Credence stares after him, as they
continue to serve.**

Scene 31

Ext. Main Street on the Lower East Side– Afternoon

Close on a Billywig – a small blue creature with helicopter-like wings on its head – flying high above the street.

Tina and Newt walk along the street, Tina carrying the case.

Tina **(on the verge of tears)**
I can't **believe** you didn't Obliviate that man! If there's an inquiry I'm finished!

Newt
So why would you be finished? I'm the one that's—

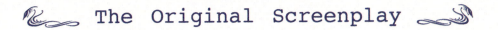

Tina
    I'm not supposed to go near the
Second Salemers!

The Billywig zooms over their heads. Newt spins, horrified, watching it.

Tina
    What was that?

Newt
    Er – moth, I think. Big moth.

Tina finds this explanation dubious. They round a corner to find a crowd gathered in front of a crumbling building. People are shouting, others are hurriedly evacuating the building. A Policeman is standing at the centre of the crowd, being harassed by disgruntled tenement-dwellers.

Jump Cut:

Newt and Tina move around the outskirts of the crowd. At the back, a tipsy Hobo is trying to attract the Policeman's attention.

Policeman
Hey ... hey – quiet down – I'm trying to get a statement ...

Housewife
... I'm telling you it's a gas explosion again, I ain't taking the kids back up there until it's safe.

Policeman
Sorry, ma'am – there ain't no smell of gas.

Hobo **(drunk)**
It warn't gas – hey, officer, I seen it! – it wuzza – a gigantic – a huge hippopotto—

Tina is looking up at the ruined building, and misses Newt sliding his wand from his sleeve and pointing it at the Hobo.

Hobo
—gas. It was gas.

The others in the crowd around him agree.

Crowd
Gas ... it was gas!

Tina again catches sight of the Billywig. Taking advantage of this distraction, Newt runs up the metal steps and inside the ruined tenement building.

Scene 32

Int. Jacob's Room— Afternoon

Newt enters Jacob's room and stops, staring: the room is completely destroyed. Footprints, broken furniture, shattered glass. Even worse: a massive hole in the opposite wall – something huge has blasted its way out. We can hear Jacob groaning from the corner.

Scene 33

Ext. Tenement Street— Afternoon

Cut back to Tina as she looks around and realises that Newt has disappeared from the crowd.

Scene 34

Int. Jacob's Room

Newt crouches beside Jacob, who lies on his back, eyes closed and moaning. Newt tries to examine a small red bite on Jacob's neck, but Jacob keeps unconsciously batting him away.

Tina **(O.S.)**
Mr Scamander!

Cut to Tina, running with purpose up the staircase of Jacob's building.

Cut back to Newt, who desperately performs a repairing charm. The room is righted, the wall

repaired, just in time before Tina enters the room.

Scene 35

Int. Jacob's Room— Afternoon

Tina hurries inside to find Newt, trying to look innocent and composed, sitting on the bed. He calmly seals the latches on his case.

Tina
  It was **open**?

Newt
  Just a smidge ...

Tina
  That crazy Niffler thing's on the loose again?

Newt
  Er – it **might** be—

Tina
>   Then look for it! Look!

Jacob moans.

Tina drops Jacob's case and makes straight for the injured Jacob.

Tina **(worried about Jacob)**
>   His neck's bleeding, he's hurt! Wake up, Mr No-Maj ...

With Tina's back turned, Newt makes towards the door. Suddenly, Tina emits a guttural scream as the Murtlap comes scuttling out from under a cabinet and latches onto her arm. Newt spins, catching the creature by the tail and grappling it into the case.

Tina
>   Mercy Lewis, what is that?

Newt
>   Nothing to worry about. That is a Murtlap.

Unnoticed by either, Jacob opens his eyes.

Tina
What else have you got in there?

Jacob (recognising Newt)
You!

Newt
Hello.

Tina
Easy, Mr—

Jacob
Kowalski ... Jacob ...

Tina takes Jacob's hand to shake it.

Newt raises his wand. Jacob recoils in fear, clutching at Tina, who moves protectively in front of him.

Tina
You can't Obliviate him! We need him as a witness.

Newt
I'm sorry – you've just yelled at me

the length of New York for not doing it in the first place . . .

Tina
He's hurt! He looks ill!

Newt
He'll be fine. Murtlap bites aren't serious.

Newt puts his wand away. Jacob retches into the corner, while Tina looks at Newt in disbelief.

Newt
I admit that is a slightly more severe reaction than I've seen, but if it was really serious – he'd have . . .

Tina
What?

Newt
Well, the first symptom would be flames out of his anus—

Terrified, Jacob feels the seat of his pants.

Tina

This is balled up!

Newt

It'll last forty-eight hours at most! I can keep him if you want me to—

Tina

Oh, keep him? We don't keep them! Mr Scamander, do you know **anything** about the wizarding community in America?

Newt

I do know a few things, actually. I know you have rather backwards laws about relations with non-magic people. That you're not meant to befriend them, that you can't marry them, which seems mildly absurd to me.

Jacob is following this conversation, open-mouthed.

Tina

Who's going to marry him? You're both coming with me—

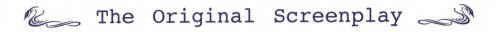

Newt
I don't see why I need to come with you—

Tina tries to lift the partially conscious Jacob from the floor.

Tina
Help me!

Newt feels obliged to help.

Jacob
I'm ... I'm dreaming, right? Yeah ... I'm tired, I never went to the bank. This is all just some big nightmare, right?

Tina
For the both of us, Mr Kowalski.

Tina and Newt Disapparate with Jacob.

We focus on the photo of Jacob's grandma, once again hanging on the wall. Eventually the photo gives a little shake before falling and revealing a hole in the wall, inhabited by the Niffler.

Scene 36

Ext. Upper East Side— Afternoon

A young boy, clutching a huge lollipop, is led down the busy street by his father. As they pass a fruit barrow, an apple suddenly levitates, bobbing along beside him. The boy gazes in wonder as the apple is eaten by something invisible, then the smile fades as his lollipop is snatched by the same unseen hands.

At a newsstand, the eyes of a lady on an advertisement blink open. The outline of a creature becomes visible, camouflage-like, before it peels away from the poster. It moves along the street, invisible again, only locatable by the lollipop

it holds – seemingly suspended in mid-air. A dog barks in its direction, and the creature scuttles on, knocking over newspaper stands, causing bikes and cars to swerve.

Angle on the roof of a department store – we see a thin blue tail slither inside a small attic window. Suddenly the building shakes and tiles break away, as the creature's size expands to fill the whole room.

Scene 37

Int. Shaw Tower Newsroom—Dusk

The glittering Art Deco headquarters of a media empire. Many journalists are hard at work in an outer office.

An elevator opens and Langdon Shaw bustles excitedly through the room, leading the Second Salemers. He carries maps, several old books and a handful of photographs.

Mary Lou is composed, Chastity looks shy and Modesty is excited, curious. Credence looks nervous – he doesn't like crowds.

Langdon
> ... and so this is the newsroom.

Langdon spins around excitedly, eager to show the Second Salemers that he holds authority here.

Langdon
> Let's go!

Langdon moves around the office and speaks to some of the workers.

Langdon
> Hey, how are you? Make way for the Barebones! Now, they're just putting the papers to bed, as they say.

Looks of veiled amusement from journalists as Langdon leads his group to double doors at the end of the open-plan area. Henry Shaw Sr's assistant – Barker – stands up, anxious.

Barker
> Mr Shaw, sir, he's with the senator—

Langdon
    Never mind that, Barker, I wanna see my father!

Langdon pushes past.

Scene 38

Int. Shaw Sr's Penthouse Office—Dusk

A large, impressive office with spectacular views across the city. The newspaper magnate – Henry Shaw Sr – is talking to his elder son, Senator Shaw.

Senator Shaw
    ... we could just buy the boats ...

The doors burst open to reveal a harassed-looking Barker and an excitable Langdon.

Barker
    I'm so sorry, Mr Shaw, but your son insisted—

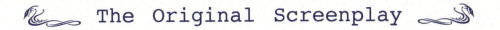

Langdon
Father, you're going to want to hear this.

Langdon moves towards his father's desk and begins spreading out photographs. We recognise some of the images: the destroyed streets from the start of the film.

Langdon
I've got something huge!

Shaw Sr
Your brother and I are busy here, Langdon. Working on his campaign. We don't have time for this.

Mary Lou, Credence, Chastity and Modesty enter the office. Shaw Sr and Senator Shaw stare. Credence stands with his head bowed, embarrassed, nervous.

Langdon
This is Mary Lou Barebone from the New Salem Philanthropic Society, and she's got a big story for you!

Shaw Sr
Oh she has – has she?

Langdon
There's strange things going on all over the city. The people behind this – they are not like you and me. This is witchcraft, don't you see?

Shaw Sr and the Senator look dubious – all too used to Langdon's harebrained little projects and interests.

Shaw Sr
Langdon.

Langdon
She doesn't want any money.

Shaw Sr
Then either her story is worthless, or she's lying about the cost. Nobody gives away anything valuable for free.

Mary Lou **(confident, persuasive)**
You are right, Mr Shaw. What we desire is infinitely more valuable than money: it's your influence. Millions of people read your newspapers and they

need to be made aware about this
danger.

Langdon
    The crazy disturbances in the
subway – just look at the pictures!

Shaw Sr
    I'd like you and your friends to leave.

Langdon
    No, you're missing a trick here. Just
look at the evidence—

Shaw Sr
    Really.

Senator Shaw **(joining his father and
brother)**
    Langdon. Just listen to Father and go.

His eyes shift, focus on Credence.

Senator Shaw
    And take the freaks with you.

**Credence perceptibly twitches,
disturbed by anger in his vicinity.
Mary Lou is calm, but steely.**

Langdon
> This is Father's office, not yours, and I'm sick of this every time I walk in here ...

Shaw Sr silences his son and motions for the Barebones to leave.

Shaw Sr
> That's it – thank you.

Mary Lou **(calm, dignified)**
> We hope you'll reconsider, Mr Shaw. We're not difficult to find. Until then, we thank you for your time.

Shaw Sr and Senator Shaw watch Mary Lou as she turns, leading her children out. The newsroom has fallen quiet, everyone craning to hear the row.

As he departs, Credence drops a leaflet. Senator Shaw moves forwards and bends to pick it up. He glances at the witches on the front.

Senator Shaw **(to Credence)**
> Hey, boy. You dropped something.

The Senator crumples up the leaflet before putting it in Credence's hand.

Senator Shaw
Here you go, freak – why don't you put that in the trash where you all belong.

Behind Credence, Modesty's eyes burn. She clutches Credence's hand protectively.

Scene 39

Ext. Brownstone Street—Shortly Afterwards—Dusk

Tina and Newt stand on either side of an ailing Jacob, trying to keep him steady.

Tina
    Take a right here ...

Jacob makes various retching sounds, the bite on his neck clearly affecting him more and more.

As the group rounds a corner, Tina hurries them to hide behind a large repair truck. From here she peers at a house across the street.

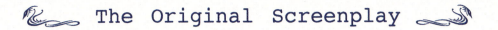

Tina

   Okay – before we go in – I'm not supposed to have men on the premises.

Newt

   In that case, Mr Kowalski and I can easily seek other accommodation—

Tina

   Oh no, you don't!

Tina quickly grabs Jacob's arm and pulls him across the road, Newt dutifully following.

Tina

   Watch your step.

Scene 40

Int. Goldstein Residence, Stairwell— Dusk

Newt, Tina and Jacob tiptoe up the stairs. They have just reached the first landing when Mrs Esposito, the landlady, calls out. The group freezes.

Mrs Esposito **(O.S.)**
  That you, Tina?

Tina
  Yes, Mrs Esposito!

Mrs Esposito **(O.S.)**
  Are you alone?

Tina
    I'm always alone, Mrs Esposito!

A beat.

Scene 41

Int. Goldstein Residence, Sitting Room—Dusk

The group enters the Goldstein apartment.

Although impoverished, the apartment is enlivened by workaday magic. An iron is working away on its own in a corner, and a clothes horse revolves clumsily on its wooden legs in front of the fire, drying an assortment of underwear. Magazines are scattered around: The Witch's Friend, Witch Chat and Transfiguration Today.

Blonde Queenie, the most beautiful girl ever to don witches'

robes, is standing in a silk slip, supervising the mending of a dress on a dressmaker's dummy. Jacob is thunderstruck.

Newt barely notices. Impatient to leave as soon as possible, he starts peeking out of the windows.

Queenie
Teenie – you brought men home?

Tina
Gentlemen, this is my sister. You want to put something on, Queenie?

Queenie (unconcerned)
Oh, sure—

She runs her wand up the dummy and the dress runs magically up her body. Jacob watches the display, dumbfounded.

Tina, frustrated, starts tidying the apartment.

Queenie
So, who are they?

Tina
That's Mr Scamander. He's committed a serious infraction of the National Statute of Secrecy—

Queenie (impressed)
He's a **criminal**?

Tina
—uh huh, and this is Mr Kowalski, he's a No-Maj—

Queenie (suddenly worried)
A No-Maj? Teen – what are you up to?

Tina
He's sick – it's a long story – Mr Scamander has lost something, I'm going to help him find it.

Jacob suddenly staggers, very sweaty and unwell. Queenie runs to him as Tina hovers, also worried.

Queenie (as Jacob falls back onto a sofa)
You need to sit down, honey. Hey—

(reading his mind)

—he hasn't eaten all day. And—

(reading his mind)

—aww, that's rough,

(reading his mind)

—he didn't get the money he wanted for his bakery. You bake, honey? I love to cook.

Newt is watching Queenie from his spot by the window, his scientific attention now aroused.

Newt
You're a Legilimens?

Queenie
Uh huh, yeah. But I always have trouble with your kind. Brits. It's the accent.

Jacob (cottoning on, appalled)
You know how to read minds?

Queenie
Aww, don't worry, honey. Most guys think what you was thinking, first time they see me.

Queenie playfully gestures towards Jacob with her wand.

Queenie
Now, you need food.

Newt looks out the window and sees a Billywig fly past – he's nervous, impatient to get out and find his creatures.

Tina and Queenie busy themselves in the kitchen. Ingredients come floating out of cupboards as Queenie enchants them into the components of a meal – carrots and apples chop themselves, pastry rolls itself and pans stir.

Queenie **(to Tina)**
Hot dog ... again?

Tina
   Don't read my mind!

Queenie
   Not a very wholesome lunch.

Tina points her wand at the cupboards. Dishes, assorted cutlery and glasses come flying out, setting themselves on the table with a little prodding from Tina's wand. Jacob, half-fascinated, half-terrified, staggers towards the table.

Angle on Newt, his hand on the doorknob.

Queenie **(artless)**
   Hey, Mr Scamander, you prefer pie or strudel?

All look at Newt who, embarrassed, removes his hand from the doorknob.

Newt
   I really don't have a preference.

Tina stares at Newt: confrontational, but also disappointed and hurt.

Jacob is already seated at the table, tucking his napkin into his shirt.

Queenie **(reading Jacob's mind)**
    You prefer strudel, huh, honey? Strudel it is.

Jacob nods with excited enthu-siasm. Queenie grins back, delighted.

With a flick of her wand, Queenie sends raisins, apples and pastry flying into the air. The concoction neatly wraps itself up into a cylindrical pie, baking on the spot, complete with ornate decoration and a dusting of sugar. Jacob takes a deep breath in: heaven.

Tina lights candles on the table – the meal is ready.

Focus on Newt's pocket, a small squeak, and Pickett pokes his head out, curious.

Tina
    Well, sit down, Mr Scamander, we're not going to poison you.

Newt, still hovering near the door, looks somewhat charmed by the situation. Jacob glares at him subtly, willing him to sit down.

Scene 42

Ext. Broadway—Night

Credence is walking alone through a worldly crowd of late-night diners and theatre-goers. Traffic roars past. He is trying to give out leaflets but is met with only incredulity and faint derision.

The Woolworth Building looms ahead. Credence glances towards it with a hint of longing. Graves stands outside, watching Credence intently. Credence spots him, hope flickering across his face. Utterly enthralled, Credence moves across the street towards Graves, barely looking where he's going – everything else is forgotten.

Scene 43

Ext. Alleyway—Night

Credence stands, head bowed, at the end of a dimly lit alleyway. Graves joins him, moving in very close to whisper, conspiratorial:

Graves
  You're upset. It's your mother again. Somebody's said something – what did they say? Tell me.

Credence
  Do you think I'm a freak?

Graves
  No – I think you're a very special young man or I wouldn't have asked you to help me now, would I?

A pause. Graves rests a hand on Credence's arm. The human contact seems to both startle and captivate Credence.

Graves
   Have you any news?

Credence
   I'm still looking. Mr Graves, if I knew whether it was a girl or boy—

Graves
   My vision showed only the child's immense power. He or she is no older than ten, and I saw this child in close proximity to your mother – she I saw so plainly.

Credence
   That could be any one of hundreds.

Graves's tone softens – he's beguiling, comforting.

Graves
   There is something else. Something I haven't told you. I saw you beside me in New York. You're the one that gains

this child's trust. You are the key – I
saw this. You want to join the wizarding
world. I want those things too, Credence.
I want them for you. So find the child.
Find the child and we'll all be free.

Scene 44

Int. Goldstein Residence, Sitting Room—Half an Hour Later—Night

The catch on Newt's case pops open. Newt reaches down and pushes it shut.

Jacob looks a little better for having eaten. He and Queenie are getting on famously.

Queenie
   The job ain't that glamorous. I mean, I spend most days making coffee, unjinxing the john ... Tina's the career girl.

   (she reads his mind)

Nah. We're orphans. Ma and Pa died of dragon pox when we were kids. Aww ...

(reading his mind)

You're sweet. But we got each other!

Jacob
Could you stop reading my mind for a second? Don't get me wrong – I love it.

Queenie giggles, delighted, captivated by Jacob.

Jacob
This meal – it's insanely good! This is what I do – I'm a cook and this is, like, the greatest meal I have ever had in my life.

Queenie **(laughing)**
Oh you slay me! I ain't never really talked to a No-Maj before.

Jacob
Really?

Queenie and Jacob gaze into each other's eyes. Newt and Tina sit opposite each other, uncomfortably silent in the presence of such affectionate behaviour.

Queenie **(to Tina)**
I am not flirting!

Tina **(embarrassed)**
I'm just saying – don't go getting attached, he's going to have to be Obliviated!

(to Jacob)

It's nothing personal.

Jacob is suddenly very pale and sweaty again, although still trying to look good for Queenie.

Queenie **(to Jacob)**
Oh, hey, you okay, honey?

Newt briskly gets up from the table and awkwardly stands behind his chair.

Newt

Miss Goldstein, I think Mr Kowalski could do with an early night. And besides, you and I will need to be up early tomorrow morning to find my Niffler, so—

Queenie **(to Tina)**

What's a Niffler?

Tina looks put out.

Tina

Don't ask.

(moving towards a back room)

Okay, you guys can bunk in here.

Scene 45

Int. Goldstein Residence, Bedroom—Night

The boys are tucked up in neatly made twin beds. Newt is resolutely turned away on his side, while Jacob is sitting up in bed, trying to make sense of a wizarding book.

Tina, wearing patterned blue pyjamas, tentatively knocks on the door, and enters carrying a tray of cocoa. The mugs are stirring themselves – Jacob is captivated again.

Tina
    I thought you might like a hot drink?

Tina carefully hands Jacob his mug. Newt remains turned away, feigning sleep, so Tina, with some frustration, pointedly places his cup on the bedside table.

Jacob
    Hey, Mr Scamander—

(to Newt, trying to make him friendlier)

    Look, cocoa!

Newt does not move.

Tina **(irritated)**
    The toilet's down the hall to the right.

Jacob
    Thanks ...

As Tina shuts the door, Jacob gets a quick glimpse of Queenie in the other room, wearing a much less demure dressing gown.

Jacob
    Very much ...

The moment the door closes Newt jumps up, still wearing his overcoat, and places his case on the floor. To Jacob's utter astonishment, Newt opens the case and walks down inside it, now completely out of sight.

Jacob lets out a small scream of alarm.

Newt's hand appears from the case, beckoning him imperiously. Jacob stares, breathing heavily, trying to process the situation.

Newt's hand, impatient, appears again.

Newt (O.S.)
Come on.

Jacob rallies himself, gets out of bed and steps down into Newt's case. However, he gets stuck at his waistline and tries hard to squeeze himself through, the case bouncing up and down with his efforts.

Jacob

    For the love of ...

With a final frustrated jump, Jacob suddenly disappears through the case, which snaps shut after him.

Scene 46

Int. Newt's Case—a Moment Later—Night

Jacob crashes down the steps of the case, colliding with various objects, instruments and bottles as he goes.

He finds himself inside a small wooden shed containing a camp bed, tropical gear and various tools hung up on the walls. Wooden cupboards contain rope, nets and collecting jars. A very old typewriter, a pile of manuscripts and a medieval bestiary sit on a desk. Potted plants line a shelf. Rows of pills and tablets, syringes and vials form a medicine chest, and tacked up on the walls are notes, maps, drawings and a few

**moving photographs of extra-
ordinary creatures. A dried carcass
hangs from a hook. Several sacks
of feed are resting against
the wall.**

Newt **(glances at Jacob)**
Will you sit down.

**Jacob drops onto a crate hand-
labelled Mooncalf Pellets.**

Jacob
That's good.

**Newt moves forward to examine
the bite on Jacob's neck – one quick
glance.**

Newt
Ah, that's definitely the Murtlap. You
must be particularly susceptible. See,
you're a Muggle. So our physiologies are
subtly different.

**Newt busies himself at his work
station, using plants and the contents
of various bottles to create a poultice,**

which he rapidly applies to Jacob's neck.

Jacob
  Oww ...

Newt
  Now stay still. Now that should stop the sweating.

(handing him some pills)

And one of those should sort the twitch.

Jacob looks suspiciously at the pills in his hand. Finally, deciding he has nothing to lose, he swallows them.

Angle on Newt, who has now removed his waistcoat, undone his bow tie and lowered his braces. He picks up a meat cleaver and hacks chunks of meat off a large carcass, before tossing them into a bucket.

Newt **(handing him the bucket)**
  Take that.

Jacob looks disgusted. Newt doesn't notice, his attention now focused on a spiny cocoon, which he slowly begins to squeeze. As he does so, the cocoon emits a luminous venom, which Newt collects into a glass vial.

Newt **(to the cocoon)**
Come on ...

Jacob
What you got there?

Newt
Well this – the locals call 'Swooping Evil' – not the friendliest of names. It's quite an agile fellow.

As if to demonstrate, Newt flicks the cocoon, which unravels, dangling elegantly from his finger.

Newt
I've been studying him. And I am pretty sure his venom could be quite useful if properly diluted. Just to remove bad memories, you know.

Quite suddenly Newt throws the Swooping Evil towards Jacob. The creature bursts out from its cocoon – a bat-like, spikey and colourful creature – which howls in Jacob's face before Newt recalls it. Jacob recoils dramatically, but this was evidently Newt's idea of a little joke ...

Newt **(smiling to himself)**
Probably shouldn't let him loose in here, though.

Newt opens the door of his shed and walks through.

Newt
Come on.

Jacob, now thoroughly startled, follows him out.

Scene 47

Int. Newt's Case, Animal Area—Day

The perimeter of the leather case is dimly visible, but the place has swollen to the size of a small aircraft hangar. It contains what appears to be a safari park in miniature. Each of Newt's creatures has its own perfect, magically realised, habitat.

Jacob steps into this world, totally amazed.

Newt is standing in the nearest habitat – a slice of Arizona desert. This area contains Frank, a magnificent Thunderbird – a creature like a large albatross, his glorious wings shimmering with

cloud- and sun-like patterns.
One of his legs is rubbed raw
and bloody – he has obviously
previously been chained. As
Frank flaps his wings, his habitat
fills with a torrential downpour,
thunder and lightning. Newt
uses his wand to create a magical
umbrella, shielding him from
the rain.

Newt (eyes on Frank up high)
Come on ... come on ... down you
come ... come on.

Slowly Frank calms himself,
lowering down to stand on a large
rock in front of Newt. As he does, the
rain dies down and is replaced by a
brilliant, hot sunshine.

Newt puts his wand away and
produces a handful of grubs from his
pocket. Frank watches intently.

Newt strokes Frank with his free
hand, calming him, affectionate.

Newt
Oh, thank Paracelsus. If you'd
have got out that could have been
quite catastrophic.

(to Jacob)

You see, he's the real reason I came
to America. To bring Frank home.

**Jacob, still staring, steps slowly
forwards. In reaction, Frank starts to
flap his wings, agitated.**

Newt (to Jacob)
No sorry – stay there – he's a wee
bit sensitive to strangers.

(to Frank, calming)

Here you are – here you are.

(to Jacob)

He was trafficked, you see. I found
him in Egypt, he was all chained up.
Couldn't leave him there, had to bring
him back. I'm going to put you back

where you belong, aren't I, Frank. To the wilds of Arizona.

Newt, his face full of hope and expectation, hugs Frank's head. Then, grinning, he casts the handful of grubs high into the air. Frank soars majestically upwards after them, sunlight bursting from his wings.

Newt watches him fly with love and pride. Then he turns, puts his hands to his mouth, and roars beast-like towards another area of the case.

Newt moves past Jacob, grabbing the bucket of meat. Jacob stumbles after him as several Doxys buzz around his head. Jacob, dazed, swats them out of the way. Behind him a large dung beetle rolls a giant ball of dung.

We hear Newt roar loudly again. Jacob hurries towards the sound, finding Newt in a sandy, moonlit territory.

Newt (under his breath)
Ah – here they come.

Jacob
Here who comes?

Newt
The Graphorns.

A large creature comes charging into sight: a Graphorn – built like a sabre-toothed tiger but with slimy tentacles at its mouth. Jacob screams and tries to back off, but Newt grabs hold of his arm, stopping him.

Newt
You're all right. You're all right.

The Graphorn moves closer to Newt.

Newt (stroking the Graphorn)
Hello, hello!

The Graphorn's strange slimy tentacles rest on Newt's shoulder, seeming to embrace him.

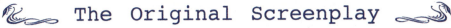

Newt
    So they're the last breeding pair in existence. If I hadn't managed to rescue them, that could have been the end of Graphorns – for ever.

A younger Graphorn trots straight up to Jacob and begins licking his hand, circling him curiously. He stares down at it, then gently reaches out and strokes its head. Newt watches Jacob, pleased.

Newt
    All right.

Newt throws a piece of meat into the enclosure, which is hastily chased and consumed by the young Graphorn.

Jacob
    So what – you, you rescue these creatures?

Newt
    Yes, that's right. Rescue, nurture and protect them, and I'm gently trying to educate my fellow wizards about them.

A tiny bright pink bird, the Fwooper, flies past and comes to rest on a little perch, suspended from mid-air.

Newt heads up a small ramp of stairs.

Newt **(to Jacob)**
  Come on.

They enter a bamboo wood, ducking and diving through the trees. Newt calls out.

Newt
  Titus? Finn? Poppy, Marlow, Tom?

They emerge into a sunlit glade, Newt producing Pickett from his pocket and holding him perched on his hand.

Newt **(to Jacob)**
  He had a cold. He needed some body warmth.

Jacob
  Aww.

They move towards a small tree bathed in sunlight. At their approach, a clan of Bowtruckles chatters and rushes out of the leaves.

Newt extends his arm towards the tree, trying to persuade Pickett to rejoin the others. The Bowtruckles clack noisily when they see Pickett.

Newt
    Right, on you hop.

Pickett steadfastly refuses to leave Newt's arm.

Newt **(to Jacob)**
    See, he has some attachment issues.

(to Pickett)

Now come on, Pickett. Pickett. No, they're not going to bully you ... now, come on. Pickett!

Pickett clings by his spindly hands to one of Newt's fingers, desperate not to return to the tree. Newt finally resigns himself.

Newt
All right. But that is exactly why they accuse me of favouritism ...

Newt puts Pickett onto his shoulder and turns. On seeing a large, round, empty nest, he looks concerned.

Newt
I wonder where Dougal's gone.

From within a nearby nest, we hear chirping sounds.

Newt
All right I'm coming ... I'm coming, Mum's here – Mum's here.

Newt reaches into the nest and scoops up a baby Occamy.

Newt
Ah – hello you – let me take a look at you.

Jacob
I know these guys.

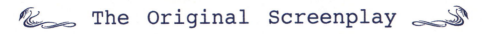

Newt
New Occamy.

(to Jacob)

Your Occamy.

Jacob
What do you mean? My Occamy?

Newt
Yes – do you want to ...

Newt proffers the Occamy to Jacob.

Jacob
Oh wow ... yeah, sure. Okay ... ah ha.

Jacob holds the newborn creature gently in his hands and stares. As he moves to stroke its head, the Occamy moves to nip him. Jacob starts backwards.

Newt
Ah, no, sorry – don't pet them. They learn to defend themselves early. See,

their shells are made of silver so they're incredibly valuable.

Newt feeds the other babies in the nest.

Jacob
Okay ...

Newt
Their nests tend to get ransacked by hunters.

Newt, delighted by Jacob's interest in his creatures, takes back the baby Occamy, placing it in the nest.

Jacob
Thank you.

(croaky)

Mr Scamander?

Newt
Call me Newt.

Jacob
Newt ... I don't think I'm dreaming.

Newt **(vaguely amused)**
What gave it away?

Jacob
I ain't got the brains to make this up.

Newt looks at Jacob, both intrigued and flattered.

Newt
Actually, would you mind throwing some of those pellets in with the Mooncalves over there?

Jacob
Yeah, sure.

Jacob bends down and picks up the bucket of pellets.

Newt
Just over there . . .

Newt grabs a nearby wheelbarrow and sets off further into the case.

Newt **(annoyed)**
Bugger – the Niffler's gone. Of course

he has, little bugger. Any chance to get his hands on something shiny.

As Jacob walks through the case, we see what appear to be golden 'leaves' falling from a tiny tree, which move together en masse towards the camera. They swarm upwards, mingling with Doxys, Glow Bugs and Grindylows which float through the air.

The camera pans up to reveal another magnificent creature, the Nundu – looking almost exactly like a lion, it has a large mane which bursts forth when it roars. It stands proudly on a large rock, roaring at the moon. Newt scatters food at its feet and purposefully moves on.

A Diricawl – a small, plump bird – waddles in the foreground followed by its constantly Apparating chicks, as Jacob climbs up a steep grassy bank.

Jacob **(to himself)**
What did you do today, Jacob? I was inside a suitcase.

At the top, Jacob finds a large moonlit rock face populated by little Mooncalves – shy, with huge eyes filling their whole faces.

Jacob
  Hey! Oh, hello fellas – all right – all right.

The Mooncalves jump and hop down the rocks towards Jacob, who finds himself suddenly surrounded by their friendly, hopeful faces.

Jacob
  Take it easy – take it easy.

As he throws pellets, the Mooncalves bob eagerly up and down. Jacob visibly seems to be feeling better – he really likes this ...

Angle on Newt, now cradling a luminescent creature with sprouting alien-like tendrils. He feeds the creature with a bottle, while carefully watching how Jacob handles the Mooncalves – he recognises a kindred spirit.

Jacob **(still feeding the Mooncalves)**
There you go, cutie. Ah, there it is.

A kind of icy cry echoes from nearby.

Jacob **(towards Newt)**
Did you hear that?

But Newt is gone. Jacob turns to see a curtain billowing open, behind which is revealed a snowscape.

We push inwards, towards a small oleaginous black mass suspended in mid-air – an Obscurus. Jacob, intrigued, moves into the snowscape to get a closer look. The mass continues to swirl, emitting a disturbed, restless energy. Jacob reaches out to touch it.

Newt **(O.S.) (sharp)**
Step back.

Jacob jumps.

Jacob
Jeez ...

Newt
>   Step back ...

Jacob
>   What's the matter with this?

Newt
>   I said step away.

Jacob
>   What the hell is this thing?

Newt
>   It's an Obscurus.

Jacob looks at Newt, who is momentarily lost in a bad reverie. Newt turns abruptly away and heads back towards the hut, his tone colder, more efficient, no longer happy to play about in the case.

Newt
>   I need to get going, find everyone who's escaped before they get hurt.

The pair enters another forest, Newt ploughing ahead, on a mission.

Jacob
    Before **they** could get hurt?

Newt
    Yes, Mr Kowalski. See, they're currently in alien terrain, surrounded by millions of the most vicious creatures on the planet.

(a beat)

Humans.

Newt stops once more, staring into a large savannah enclosure, which is empty of any beasts.

Newt
    So where would you say that a medium-sized creature that likes broad, open plains – trees – water holes – that kind of thing – where might she go?

Jacob
    In New York City?

Newt
    Yes.

Jacob
    Plains?

**Jacob shrugs as he tries to think
of somewhere.**

Jacob
    Ah – Central Park?

Newt
    And where is that exactly?

Jacob
    Where is Central Park?

A beat.

Jacob
    Well look, I would come and show
    you, but, don't you think it's kind of a
    double cross? The girls take us in –
    they make us hot cocoa . . .

Newt
    You do realise that when they see
    you've stopped sweating, they'll Obliviate
    you in a heartbeat.

Jacob
    What does 'Bliviate' mean?

Newt
    It'll be like you wake up and all memory of magic is gone.

Jacob
    I won't remember any of this?

He looks around. This world is extraordinary.

Newt
    No.

Jacob
    All right, yeah – okay – I'll help you.

Newt **(picking up a bucket)**
    Come on, then.

Scene 48

Ext./Int. Street Outside Second Salem Church—Night

Credence walks home towards the church. He looks happier than before: his meeting with Graves has comforted him.

Credence slowly enters the church, shutting the double doors quietly.

Chastity is in the kitchen area, drying crockery.

Mary Lou sits in semi-darkness on the stairs. Credence senses her and pauses, his face one of trepidation.

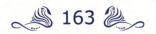

Mary Lou
Credence – where have you been?

Credence
I was ... looking for a place for tomorrow's meeting. There's a corner on Thirty-second that could—

Credence moves round to the bottom of the stairs, falling silent at the severe expression on Mary Lou's face.

Credence
I'm sorry, Ma. I didn't realise it was so late.

As if on autopilot, Credence removes his belt. Mary Lou stands and extends her hand, taking the belt. In silence, she turns and walks up the stairs, Credence obediently following.

Modesty moves to the bottom of the stairs, watching them go, a look of fear and upset on her face.

Scene 49

Ext. Central Park— Night

A large frozen pond in the middle of Central Park. Children ice-skate. A boy takes a tumble. A girl comes to help him up, they link hands.

As they are about to stand, a light becomes visible underneath the ice. A deep rumbling sound echoes. The children stare as a glowing beast glides under the ice beneath them, and off into the distance.

Scene 50

Ext. Diamond District—Night

Newt and Jacob walk along another deserted street on the way to Central Park. The shops around them are full of expensive jewellery, diamonds, precious stones. Newt, carrying his case, scans the shadows for small movements.

Newt
I was watching you at dinner.

Jacob
Yeah.

Newt
People like you, don't they, Mr Kowalski.

Jacob (startled)
Oh – well, I'm – I'm sure people like you, too – huh?

Newt (not very concerned)
No, not really. I annoy people.

Jacob (not sure how to answer)
Ah.

Newt seems thoroughly intrigued by Jacob.

Newt
Why did you decide to be a baker?

Jacob
Ah, well, um – because I'm dying – in that canning factory.

(off Newt's look)

Everyone there's dying. It just crushes the life outta you. You like canned food?

Newt
No.

Jacob

Me neither. That's why I want to make pastries, you know. It makes people happy. We're going this way.

Jacob heads off to his right. Newt follows.

Newt

So did you get your loan?

Jacob

Er, no – I ain't got no collateral. Stayed in the army too long, apparently – I don't know.

Newt

What, you fought in the war?

Jacob

Of course I fought in the war, everyone fought in the war – you didn't fight in the war?

Newt

I worked mostly with dragons, Ukrainian Ironbellies – Eastern Front.

Newt suddenly stops. He has noticed a small shiny earring lying on top of a car bonnet. His eyes move downwards: diamonds are scattered across the pavement, leading towards the window of one particular diamond shop.

Newt stealthily follows the trail, creeping past shop windows. Something catches his eye and suddenly he pauses. Very slowly, he tiptoes backwards.

The Niffler is standing in a shop window. In order to hide, it is emulating a jewellery stand, little arms outstretched, covered in diamonds.

Newt stares at the Niffler in disbelief. Sensing Newt's stare, the Niffler slowly turns. The two of them make eye contact.

A beat.

Suddenly the Niffler is off: scurrying further into the shop and away from Newt. Newt whips out his wand.

Newt

Finestra.

The window glass shatters and Newt leaps inside, seizing at drawers and cupboards, desperate to find the creature.

Jacob stares down the street, incredulous as he watches Newt who, from an outsider's perspective, appears to be looting the diamond shop.

The Niffler appears, scurrying over Newt's shoulders in an attempt to get higher and away from his clutches. Newt jumps onto a desk after him, but the Niffler is now balancing on a crystal chandelier.

Newt reaches out and trips, both he and the Niffler now hanging from the chandelier as it swings wildly round and round.

Jacob looks around the street nervously, checking if anyone else can hear the chaos coming from within the shop.

Finally the chandelier crashes to the floor, smashing. Straight away the Niffler is back up, clambering across cases full of jewellery, Newt in hot pursuit.

A catch opens on Newt's case and a roar comes from within. Jacob fearfully looks towards the case.

The Niffler and Newt continue their chase, finally climbing onto a jewellery case that can't take their weight. The case, with them both on top, falls to rest against one of the shop windows. Both Newt and the Niffler become very still ...

Jacob breathes deeply and slowly moves forward to close the latch on the case.

Suddenly a crack appears on the window. Newt watches as the crack spreads across the pane of glass and the window bursts open, shattering across the pavement – Newt and the Niffler crashing to the ground.

The Niffler is still only for a moment before running off down the street. Newt quickly gathers himself, drawing his wand.

Newt
Accio!

In slow motion the Niffler sails backwards through the air towards Newt. As he flies, he looks sideways at the most glorious window display yet. His eyes widen. Jewellery falls from his pouch as he flies towards Newt and Jacob, who duck and dive as they run forwards towards the creature.

Passing a lamp-post, the Niffler stretches out an arm, spinning around the pole and flying onwards, out of the trajectory Newt had him on, and towards the glorious window.

Newt casts a spell towards the window, turning it into a sticky jelly, which finally traps the Niffler.

Newt **(to the Niffler)**
All right? Happy?

Newt, now covered in jewellery, pulls the Niffler from the window.

We hear police sirens in the background.

Newt
    One down, two to go.

Police cars come racing through the streets.

Newt once again sets about shaking all the diamonds from the Niffler's pocket.

The police cars pull up, and Policemen run out, guns aimed at Newt and Jacob. Jacob, also covered in jewels, holds up his hands in surrender.

Jacob
    They went that way, officer ...

Police Officer 1
    Hands up!

The Niffler, stuffed into Newt's overcoat, pokes out its little nose and squeaks.

Police Officer 2
What the hell is **that**?

Jacob suddenly looks to the left, his face one of terror.

Jacob **(barely able to speak)**
Lion ...

A beat and then, in unison, the police turn both their eyes and their guns towards the other end of the street.

Perplexed, Newt looks too ... a lion is stalking towards them.

Newt **(calm)**
You know, New York is considerably more interesting than I'd expected.

Before the police can look back, Newt grabs Jacob and they Disapparate.

Scene 51

Ext. Central Park— Night

Newt and Jacob hurry through the frost-covered park.

As they cross a bridge, they are almost bowled over by an ostrich, which tears past them, running for its life.

A loud rumble can be heard in the distance.

Newt tugs protective headgear out of his pocket, and hands it to Jacob.

Newt
    Put this on.

Jacob

Why – why would I have to wear something like this?

Newt

Because your skull is susceptible to breakage under immense force.

Newt runs on. Utterly terrified, Jacob puts on the hat and chases after Newt.

Scene 52

Ext. Goldstein Residence—Night

Tina and Queenie lean out of their bedroom window, craning into the dark. Another bellowing roar reverberates through the winter night. Other windows open, neighbours stare sleepily over the city.

Scene 53

Int. Goldstein Residence—Night

Tina and Queenie burst into the bedroom where Jacob and Newt are meant to be asleep. Every trace of the two men has gone. Furious, Tina storms off to dress. Queenie looks upset.

Queenie
But we made 'em cocoa ...

Scene 54

Ext. Central Park Zoo—Night

Newt and Jacob run up to the now half-empty zoo, the outer walls of which have been demolished in places. A large pile of rubble lies at the entrance.

Another bellowing roar echoes around the brick building. Newt produces a body protector.

Newt
    Okay, if you just, uh, pop this on.

Newt stands behind Jacob, fastening the breastplate over him.

Jacob
　Okay.

Newt
　Now there's absolutely nothing for
you to worry about.

Jacob
　Tell me – has anyone ever believed
you when you told them not to worry?

Newt
　My philosophy is that worrying means
you suffer twice.

Jacob digests Newt's 'wisdom'.

**Newt picks up his case and Jacob
follows him, stumbling over rubble
and debris.**

**They stand at the entrance to the
zoo. A loud snort comes from within.**

Newt
　She's in season. She needs to mate.

**Angle on the Erumpent – a
large, rotund, rhino-like creature with**

a massive horn protruding from her forehead. Five times his size, she is nuzzling up against the enclosure of a terrified hippo.

Newt takes out a tiny vial of liquid – he pulls the stopper out with his teeth and spits it to the side before dabbing a spot of the liquid onto each wrist. Jacob looks at him – the smell is pungent.

Newt
    Erumpent musk – she is mad for it.

Newt passes Jacob the open bottle and heads into the zoo.

    Time Cut:

Newt places his case down on the ground near the Erumpent and slowly, seductively, opens it.

He begins to perform a 'mating ritual' – a series of grunts, wiggles, rolls and groans – to gain the Erumpent's attention.

Finally the Erumpent turns away from the hippo – she is interested in Newt. They face each other, circle round, undulating weirdly. The Erumpent's demeanour is puppy-like, her horn glowing orange.

Newt rolls along the floor – the Erumpent copies, moving nearer and nearer to the open case.

Newt
Good girl – come on – into the case ...

Jacob takes a sniff of the Erumpent musk. As he does so, a fish flies through the air and jolts him, spilling the musk.

The wind changes. Trees rustle. The Erumpent takes a deep breath in – she can smell the new, more powerful aroma coming from Jacob.

Jacob looks around. A seal sits behind him looking guilty, before cheekily running away.

When Jacob turns back, he sees the Erumpent is now on her feet, staring at him.

Angle on Newt and Jacob, realising what is about to happen.

Back to Scene:

The Erumpent charges towards the source of the smell, bellowing madly. Jacob wails, running as fast as he can in the opposite direction. The Erumpent gives chase – they crash through rubble and ice-ponds, before charging across the snow-covered park.

Newt draws his wand—

Newt
    Repar—

Before he can finish, his wand is whipped out of his hand by a baboon, which runs off, clutching its prize.

Newt
    Merlin's beard!

Angle on Jacob, tanking along, the Erumpent close behind him.

Angle on Newt, face to face with the curious baboon, which examines his wand.

Newt breaks a bit of twig from a branch and holds it out, trying to persuade the baboon to trade with him.

Newt
They're exactly the same ... same thing.

Back to Jacob:

In trying to climb a tree, Jacob has ended up hanging precariously upside down from a branch.

Jacob
(bellowing, terrified)

Newt!

We see the Erumpent below him. She lies on her back, wiggling her legs in the air invitingly.

Angle back on Newt – the baboon shakes Newt's wand.

Newt
No, no, no, don't!

Newt looks worried – bang – the wand 'goes off', the spell knocking the baboon backwards. The wand flies back to Newt.

Newt
I'm so sorry—

Angle on Jacob – the Erumpent is now on her feet. She charges towards the tree, digging her horn deep into the trunk. The tree bubbles with glowing liquid before exploding and crashing to the ground.

Jacob is thrown off, rolling down a steep, snowy hill and onto the frozen lake below.

The Erumpent charges after him, hits the ice and skids.

Newt comes careering down the hill, also hitting the ice. He performs an athletic slide, his case open – the Erumpent is mere feet from Jacob when the case swallows her.

Newt
Good show, Mr Kowalski!

Jacob holds out his hand to shake.

Jacob
Call me Jacob.

They shake hands.

Third Person POV: Someone watches as Newt hauls Jacob up and they slip and slide across the frozen lake as fast as they can.

Newt
Well, two down, one to go.

Hold on Tina as she hides on the bridge above them, peeking down.

Newt **(O.S.) (to Jacob)**
In you hop.

We see the case sitting alone
below the bridge.

Tina quickly appears around
the corner and hurriedly sits on the
case. She closes the catches, looking
shocked but determined.

Announcer (V.O.)
  Ladies and gentlemen ...

Scene 55

Int. City Hall—Night

A large ornately decorated hall, covered in patriotic emblems. Hundreds of glamorously dressed people sit at round tables, looking towards a stage at the far end. Over this stage hangs a large poster of Senator Shaw with a slogan reading ``America's Future'.

An Announcer stands behind the microphone.

Announcer
    ... now tonight's keynote speaker needs no introduction from me.
He's been mentioned as a future

President – and if you don't believe me, just read his daddy's newspapers—

Indulgent laughter from the crowd. We see Shaw Sr and Langdon seated at a table, surrounded by the crème de la crème of New York society.

Announcer
—ladies and gentlemen, I give you the Senator for New York, Henry Shaw!

Tumultuous applause. Senator Shaw bounds forwards, acknowledging the cheers, pointing and winking at intimates in the crowd, and mounts the steps.

Scene 56

Ext. Dark Street—Night

Something is streaking through the streets, too large and fast for a human. Strange, laboured breathing and snarling – it is inhuman, beast-like.

Scene 57

Ext. Street Near City Hall—Night

Tina is hurrying along, clutching the case. Street lights start going out around her. She stops, feels something pass in the darkness – turns, staring, scared.

Scene 58

Int. City Hall—Night

Senator Shaw
    ... and it's true we have made some progress, but there is no reward for idleness. So just as the odious saloons have been banished ...

A strange, haunting noise comes from the organ pipes at the back of the room. Everyone turns to look, the Senator pauses.

Senator Shaw
    ... so now the pool halls, and these private parlours ...

The strange noise gets louder.

Guests turn to look again. The Senator seems anxious. People mutter.

Suddenly something explodes forth from underneath the organ. Something huge and bestial, although invisible, is soaring down the hall – tables fly, people are thrown, lights smash and people scream as it carves a line towards the stage.

Senator Shaw is thrown backwards against his own poster, raised up high and suspended for a moment in mid-air before being brought down with a violent crash – dead.

The 'beast' rips at his poster – a frenzied slashing with harsh, noisy breathing – before swarming back out from where it came.

Sounds of anguish and panic from the crowd as Shaw Sr fights through the debris towards his son's torn and bleeding body.

Angle on Senator Shaw's body, his face brutally scarred. Shaw Sr looks devastated as he crouches beside his son.

Angle on Langdon, now on his feet, slightly drunk. Determined, perhaps triumphant.

Langdon
Witches!

Scene 59

Int. Macusa Lobby— Night

Focus on the gigantic dial showing the Magical Exposure Threat Level. The hand moves from Severe to Emergency.

Tina, case in hand, runs up the lobby steps, past witches and wizards huddled in groups, whispering nervously.

Heinrich Eberstadt **(V.O.)**
Our American friends have permitted a breach of the Statute of Secrecy . . .

Scene 60

Int. Pentagram Office—Night

An impressive hall arranged like an old parliament debating chamber. Every seat is occupied by wizards from all parts of the world. Madam Picquery is presiding, Graves at her side.

The Swiss delegate is speaking.

Heinrich Eberstadt
    ... that threatens to expose us all.

Madam Picquery
    I will not be lectured by the man who let Gellert Grindelwald slip through his fingers—

A hologram image of Senator Shaw's dead and twisted body floats high above the room, emitting a glowing light.

All heads turn as Tina hurries into the chamber.

Tina
    Madam President, I'm so sorry to interrupt, but this is critical—

Echoing silence. Tina slides to a halt in the middle of the marble floor before realising exactly what she's walked into. The delegates stare at her.

Madam Picquery
    You'd better have an excellent excuse for this intrusion, Miss Goldstein.

Tina
    Yes – I do.

(stepping forwards to address her)

    Ma'am. Yesterday a wizard entered New York with a case. This case of

magical creatures, and – unfortunately – some have escaped.

Madam Picquery
He arrived yesterday? You have known for twenty-four hours that an unregistered wizard set magical beasts loose in New York and you see fit to tell us only when a man has been killed?

Tina
Who has been killed?

Madam Picquery
Where is this man?

Tina sets the case flat on the floor and thumps the lid. After a second or two, it creaks open. First Newt, then Jacob emerge, looking sheepish and nervous.

British Envoy
Scamander?

Newt **(closing the case)**
Oh – er – hello, Minister.

Momolu Wotorson
Theseus Scamander? The war hero?

British Envoy
No, this is his little brother. And what in the name of Merlin are you doing in New York?

Newt
I came to buy an Appaloosa Puffskein, sir.

British Envoy (suspicious)
Right. What are you really doing here?

Madam Picquery (to Tina, about Jacob)
Goldstein – and who is this?

Tina
This is Jacob Kowalski, Madam President, he's a No-Maj who got bitten by one of Mr Scamander's creatures.

Furious reaction from the Macusa employees and dignitaries all around.

Ministers **(whispers)**
No-Maj? Obliviated?

Newt is absorbed in the image of Senator Shaw's body floating around the room.

Newt
Merlin's beard!

Madam Ya Zhou
You know which of your creatures was responsible, Mr Scamander?

Newt
No creature did this ... don't pretend! You must know what that was, look at the marks ...

Angle on Senator Shaw's face.

Angle on Newt.

Newt
That was an Obscurus.

Mass consternation, muttering, exclamations. Graves looks alert.

Madam Picquery
      You go too far, Mr Scamander.

      There is no Obscurial in America.
Impound that case, Graves!

      Graves summons the case; it
lands next to him. Newt draws his
wand.

Newt **(to Graves)**
      No ... give that b—!

Madam Picquery
      Arrest them!

      A dazzling eruption of spells hit
Newt, Tina and Jacob, all of whom
are slammed to their knees. Newt's
wand flies out of his hand, caught by
Graves.

      Graves stands and picks up the
case.

Newt **(magically restrained)**
      No – no – don't hurt those creatures –
please, you don't understand – nothing in
there is dangerous, nothing!

Madam Picquery
We'll be the judges of that!

(to the Aurors now standing behind them)

Take them to the cells!

Angle on Graves watching Tina as she, Newt and Jacob are dragged away.

Newt **(screaming, desperate)**
Don't hurt those creatures – there is nothing in there that is dangerous. Please don't hurt my creatures – they are not dangerous ... please, they are not dangerous!

Scene 61

Int. Macusa Cell—Day

Newt, Tina and Jacob sitting, Newt with his head in his hands, still in utter despair about his creatures. Finally Tina, on the verge of tears, breaks the silence.

Tina
    I am so sorry about your creatures, Mr Scamander. I truly am.

Newt remains silent.

Jacob **(sotto voce, to Tina)**
    Can someone please tell me what this Obscurial Obscurius thing is? Please?

Tina **(also sotto voce)**
There hasn't been one for centuries—

Newt
I met one in Sudan three months ago. There used to be more of them but they still exist. Before wizards went underground, when we were still being hunted by Muggles, young wizards and witches sometimes tried to suppress their magic to avoid persecution. Instead of learning to harness or to control their powers, they developed what was called an Obscurus.

Tina **(off Jacob's confusion)**
It's an unstable, uncontrollable dark force that busts out and – and attacks ... and then vanishes ...

As she talks, we see the penny dropping. An Obscurus fits everything she knows about the perpetrator of the New York attacks.

Tina **(to Newt)**
Obscurials can't survive long, can they?

Newt
There's no documented case of any Obscurial surviving past the age of ten. The one I met in Africa was eight when she – she was eight when she died.

Jacob
What are you telling me here – that Senator Shaw was killed by a – by a **kid**?

Newt's look says 'yes'.

Scene 62

Int. Second Salem Church, Main Hall— Day—Montage

Modesty approaches the long table at which many orphan children sit hungrily eating.

Modesty **(continuing her chant)**
... my momma, your momma, flying on a switch,

My momma, your momma, witches never cry,

My momma, your momma, witches gonna die!

Modesty gathers several of the children's leaflets from the table.

Modesty
    Witch number one,
drown in a river!

    Witch number two,
gotta noose to give her!

    Witch number three ...

Time Cut:

The children, having finished their meal, leave the table with their leaflets and head for the door.

Chastity **(calling after them)**
    Hand out your leaflets! I'll know if you dump 'em. Tell me if you see anything suspicious.

Close on Credence – he's washing dishes, but watching the children intently.

Modesty follows the last of the children out of the church.

Scene 63

Ext. Street Outside Second Salem Church— Day

Modesty stands in the middle of the busy street. She throws her leaflets high into the air, watching with glee as they fall around her.

Scene 64

Int. Macusa Cell/ Corridor—Day

Two Executioners in white coats lead a shackled Newt and Tina down to a dark basement, away from the cell.

Newt turns to look back.

Newt **(over his shoulder)**
It was good to make your acquaintance, Jacob, and I hope you get your bakery.

Angle on Jacob, scared, left behind, clutching at the bars of the cell. He waves forlornly after Newt.

Scene 65

Int. Interrogation Room—Day

A small, bare room, black-walled and windowless.

Graves sits opposite Newt at an interrogation desk, a file open in front of him. Newt squints forward, a bright light shining into his eyes.

Tina stands behind, flanked by the two Executioners.

Graves
  You're an interesting man,
Mr Scamander.

Tina **(stepping forwards)**
  Mr Graves—

Graves holds a finger to his lips, signalling for Tina to be silent. The gesture is patronising, but authoritative. Tina looks kowtowed – she obeys, stepping back into the shadows.

Graves examines the file on his desk.

Graves
   You were thrown out of Hogwarts for endangering human life—

Newt
   That was an accident!

Graves
   —with a beast. Yet one of your teachers argued strongly against your expulsion. Now, what makes Albus Dumbledore so fond of you?

Newt
   I really couldn't say.

Graves
   So setting a pack of dangerous creatures loose here was just another accident, is that right?

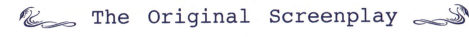

Newt
　Why would I do it deliberately?

Graves
　To expose wizardkind. To provoke war
between the magical and non-magical
worlds.

Newt
　Mass slaughter for the greater good,
you mean?

Graves
　Yes. Quite.

Newt
　I'm not one of Grindelwald's fanatics,
Mr Graves.

**A tiny change of expression
tells us that Newt has scored a hit.
Graves is looking more menacing.**

Graves
　I wonder what you can tell me about
this, Mr Scamander?

**With a slow move of his hand,
Graves raises up the Obscurus from**

Newt's case. He brings it onto the desk – it is pulsing, swirling and hissing.

Close on Tina as she stares, disbelieving.

Graves reaches a hand towards the Obscurus – he's utterly fascinated. At his sudden close proximity, the Obscurus swirls faster, bubbling and shrinking backwards.

Newt turns instinctively to Tina. Without fully realising why, it is she whom he wants to convince.

Newt
It's an Obscurus—

(off her look)

But, it's not what you think. I managed to separate it from the Sudanese girl as I tried to save her – I wanted to take it home, to study it—

(off Tina's shock)

But it cannot survive outside that
box, it could not hurt anyone, Tina!

Graves
    So it's useless without the host?

Newt
    'Useless? Useless?' That is a
parasitical magical force that killed a
child. What on earth would you use
it for?

   **Newt, anger finally boiling within
him, stares at Graves. Tina,
reacting to the atmosphere, also looks
to Graves – concern and trepidation
written across her face.**

   **Graves stands, brushing off the
questions, turning the blame back
onto Newt.**

Graves
    You fool nobody, Mr Scamander.
You brought this Obscurus into the city
of New York in the hope of causing
mass disruption, breaking the Statute
of Secrecy and revealing the magical
world—

Newt

You know that can't hurt anyone, you know that!

Graves

—you are therefore guilty of a treasonous betrayal of your fellow wizards and are sentenced to death. Miss Goldstein, who has aided and abetted you—

Newt

No, she's done nothing of the kind—

Graves

—she receives the same sentence.

The two Executioners step forwards. They calmly, intrusively, press the tips of their wands into Newt and Tina's necks.

Tina is so overcome with shock and fear that she can barely speak.

Graves (to the Executioners)

Just do it immediately. I will inform President Picquery myself.

Newt
Tina.

Graves again places a finger to his lips.

Graves
Shhhh.

(waving to the Executioners)

Please.

Scene 66

Int. Shabby Basement Meeting Room—Day

Queenie is carrying a tray of coffee and mugs towards a meeting room.

Suddenly she freezes, her eyes widen, a look of terror across her face. She drops the tray – cups smashing on the floor.

An assortment of low-level Macusa functionaries turn to stare at her. Queenie stares back, stunned, before running away down the corridor.

Scene 67

Int. Corridor Leading to Death Cell—Day

A long black metallic corridor leads into a pure white cell, which consists of a chair suspended magically over a square pool of rippling potion.

Newt and Tina are forced into this room by the Executioners. A guard stands at the door.

Tina **(to Executioner 1)**
  Don't do this – Bernadette – please—

Executioner 1
  It don't hurt.

Tina is led to the edge of the pool. She begins panicking, her breathing heavy and erratic.

The smiling Executioner 1 raises a wand and carefully extracts Tina's happy memories from her head. Tina instantly calms – her expression now vacant, other-worldly.

Executioner 1 casts the memories into the potion, which ripples, coming alive with scenes from Tina's life.

A young Tina smiles up as her mother calls.

Tina's Mother **(V.O.)**
Tina ... Tina ... come on, pumpkin – time for bed. Are you ready?

Tina
Momma ...

Tina's mother appears in the pool, her expression loving and warm. The real Tina watches, smiling down.

Executioner 1
 Don't that look good. You wanna get in? Huh?

Tina nods vacantly.

Scene 68

Int. Macusa Lobby—Day

Queenie stands in the crowded lobby. The elevator doors sound.

Angle on the elevator doors, which open revealing Jacob, escorted by Sam, the Obliviator.

Queenie hurries towards them, determined.

Queenie
Hey, Sam!

Sam
Hey, Queenie.

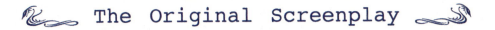

Queenie
They need you downstairs. I'll
Obliviate this guy.

Sam
You ain't qualified.

**Grim-faced, Queenie reads his
mind.**

Queenie
Hey, Sam – does Cecily know you
been seeing Ruby?

**Angle on Ruby, a Macusa witch,
standing ahead of them. She smiles
at Sam.**

**Angle on Queenie and Sam –
Sam looks nervous.**

Sam **(appalled)**
How'd you—?

Queenie
Let me Obliviate this guy
and she'll never hear about it
from me.

**Stunned, Sam backs away.
Queenie seizes Jacob's arm
and marches him off across the
cavernous lobby.**

Jacob
What are you doin'?

Queenie
Shhhh! Teen's in trouble, I'm trying
to listen—

(she reads Tina's mind)

Jacob, where's Newt's case?

Jacob

I think that guy Graves took it—

Queenie
Okay, come on—

Jacob
What? You're not gonna Obliviate
me?

Queenie
Of course not – you're one of us now!

Queenie hurries him towards the main staircase.

Scene 69

Int. Death Cell—Day

Tina sits in the execution chair. She gazes down: beneath her swirl happy images of her family, her parents, a young Queenie.

Memory:

We move into the pool and follow one of Tina's memories: Tina walks inside the Second Salem Church and up the stairs. She finds Mary Lou, standing over Credence, belt in hand – Credence looks terrified. In anger, Tina casts a spell, striking Mary Lou. Tina moves forward to comfort Credence.

Tina
   It's okay.

Angle back on real Tina, still gazing into the pool, smiling wistfully.

Angle on Newt, who glances quickly down his own arm – Pickett is clambering, quiet and agile, towards the shackles holding Newt's hands.

Scene 70

Int. Corridor Leading to Graves's Office— Day

Angle on the door to Graves's office.

Queenie **(O.S.)**
Alohomora.

We see Queenie and Jacob standing awkwardly outside Graves's office, Queenie trying desperately to open the door.

Queenie
Aberto ...

The door remains locked.

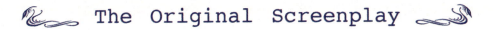

Queenie (frustrated)

Ugh. He would know a fancy spell to lock his office.

Scene 71

Int. Death Cell—Day

Back to Pickett as he finishes unlocking the shackles holding Newt's wrists, and quickly climbs onto Executioner 2's coat.

Executioner 2 **(to Newt)**
Okay, let's get the good stuff out of you—

Executioner 2 raises her wand to Newt's forehead. Newt seizes his opportunity – he jumps backwards out of the way before revealing the Swooping Evil, which he throws forwards towards the pool. He then swiftly turns and punches the guard, knocking him out cold.

The Swooping Evil has now expanded into a gigantic, spooky but weirdly beautiful butterfly-esque reptile with skeletal wings. It continues to circle round and round the pool.

Pickett clambers onto Executioner 2's arm and bites, startling and distracting her, giving Newt time to grab her arms and take aim with her wand. A spell fires, hitting Executioner 1, who drops to the floor, her wand falling into the pool. As it falls, the liquid rises up in viscous black bubbles, instantly engulfing the wand.

In reaction, Tina's memories turn from good to bad: we see Mary Lou, pointing aggressively at Tina.

Mary Lou
  Witch!

Tina, still enraptured by the pool, looks increasingly terrified. Her chair is lowering closer and closer to the liquid.

**The Swooping Evil glides across
the room, knocking Executioner 2
to the ground.**

Scene 72

Int. Corridor Leading to Graves's Office— Day

After a quick glance around, Jacob gives the door a hefty kick. It breaks open. Jacob stands guard as Queenie runs in and grabs Newt's case and Tina's wand.

Scene 73

Int. Death Cell—Day

Tina snaps out of her reverie and screams.

Tina
  Mr Scamander!

The liquid has now turned into a black bubbling death potion. It rises up, surrounding Tina on her chair. Tina stands up to get away, almost falling off in her haste. She tries desperately to regain her balance.

Newt
  Don't panic!

Tina
   What do you suggest I do instead?

   Newt makes a strange tutting sound, commanding the Swooping Evil to circle the pool once more.

Newt
   Jump ...

   Tina looks at the Swooping Evil – fearful, disbelieving.

Tina
   Are you crazy?

Newt
   Jump on him.

   Newt stands on the edge of the pool watching the Swooping Evil as it circles round and round Tina.

Newt
   Tina, listen to me. I'll catch you. Tina!

   The two make intense eye contact, Newt trying to reassure ...

The liquid has now risen up in waves to Tina's full height – she's losing sight of Newt.

Newt **(insistent, very calm)**
  I'll catch you. I've got you Tina ...

Suddenly Newt cries out.

Newt
  Go!

Tina jumps in between two of the waves, just as the Swooping Evil passes. She lands on its back, only inches away from the swirling liquid, then hops quickly forwards, straight into Newt's open arms.

For a split second Newt and Tina gaze at each other, before Newt raises his hand, recalling the Swooping Evil, which folds into a cocoon once more.

Newt grabs Tina's hand and heads for the exit.

Newt
  Come on!

Scene 74

Int. Death Cell
Corridor—Day

**Queenie and Jacob march
along the corridor with purpose.**

**An alarm goes off in the distance –
other wizards hurry past them
in the opposite direction.**

Scene 75

Int. Macusa Lobby— Minutes Later—Day

The alarm blares out across the lobby.

Confusion reigns among the crowd – people gather in groups, nervously chattering, others scurry about, urgent, anxious.

A team of Aurors hurtles across the lobby, headed directly for the stairs leading down to the basement.

Scene 76

Int. Death Cell Corridor/Basement Corridor—Day

Newt and Tina, hand in hand, charge through the basement corridors. Suddenly accosted by the group of Aurors, they turn, darting behind pillars, just missing the fired curses and spells.

Newt again sends out the Swooping Evil, which swirls overhead, flying in and out of pillars, blocking curses and knocking Aurors to the ground.

Angle on the Swooping Evil using its proboscis to probe in one of the Auror's ears.

Newt (making a clicking sound)
    Leave his brains. Come on!
Come on!

Tina and Newt run onwards, the Swooping Evil flying after, blocking curses as it goes.

Tina
    What **is** that thing?

Newt
    Swooping Evil.

Tina
    Well, I love it!

Angle on Queenie and Jacob, walking briskly through the basement. Newt and Tina sprint round the corner and almost collide with them. The four stare at one another, panic on all their faces.

Finally Queenie gestures to the case.

Queenie
    Get in!

Scene 77

Int. Stairs Leading to Cells—Moments Later—Day

Graves moves down the stairs with urgency. For the first time, a look of panic on his face.

Scene 78

Int. Macusa Lobby—
Minutes Later—Day

Queenie moves quickly across the
lobby floor, trying desperately not
to be conspicuous in her haste, but
acutely aware of the need to leave.
A flustered Abernathy emerges
from a crowd of wizards.

Abernathy
  Queenie!

Queenie, poised at the top of the
stairs, turns and composes herself.
Abernathy moves towards her,
straightening his tie, trying to appear
calm and authoritative – Queenie
obviously makes him nervous.

Abernathy **(a large smile)**
Where you going?

Queenie puts on an alluringly innocent expression and holds the case behind her back.

Queenie
I'm ... I'm sick, Mr Abernathy.

She coughs a little, widening her eyes.

Abernathy
Again? Well – what've you got there?

A beat.

Queenie thinks fast, her face quickly breaking into a breathtaking smile.

Queenie
Ladies' things.

Queenie produces the case and innocently trots up the steps towards Abernathy.

Queenie
    You wanna take a look? I don't mind.

Abernathy is overcome with embarrassment.

Abernathy **(swallowing hard)**
    Oh! Good gravy, no! I – you get well now!

Queenie **(smiling sweetly and arranging his tie)**
    Thanks!

Queenie immediately turns and hurries down the stairs leaving Abernathy – heart racing – staring after her.

Scene 79

Ext. Streets of New York—Late Afternoon

High wide above New York. We zoom over rooftops before diving down through streets and alleyways, past speeding cars and cackling children.

We come to rest in an alleyway at the Second Salem Church, where Credence is pasting up posters advertising Mary Lou's next meeting.

Graves Apparates in the alleyway. Credence, startled, backs away, but Graves makes straight for him, his tone and manner urgent, forceful.

Graves
Credence. Have you found the child?

Credence
I can't.

Graves, impatient but feigning calm, holds out his hand – suddenly seeming caring, affectionate.

Graves
Show me.

Credence whimpers and cowers, almost backing further away. Graves gently takes Credence's hand in his own and examines it – the hand is covered in deep red cuts, sore and bleeding.

Graves
Shhhh. My boy, the sooner we find this child, the sooner you can put that pain in the past where it belongs.

Graves gently, almost seductively, moves his thumb across the cuts, healing them instantly. Credence stares.

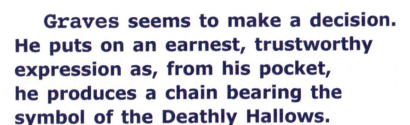

**Graves seems to make a decision.
He puts on an earnest, trustworthy
expression as, from his pocket,
he produces a chain bearing the
symbol of the Deathly Hallows.**

Graves
    I want you to have this, Credence.
I would trust very few with it—

**Graves moves close, placing the
chain around Credence's neck as he
whispers.**

Graves
    Very few.

**Graves places his hands on
either side of Credence's neck,
drawing him in, his speech quiet,
intimate.**

Graves
    ... but you – you're different.

**Credence is unsure, both
nervous of and attracted by Graves's
behaviour.**

Graves rests his hand on Credence's heart, covering the pendant.

Graves

Now, when you find the child, touch this symbol and I will know, and I will come to you.

Graves moves even closer to Credence, his face inches from the boy's neck – the effect is both alluring and threatening – as he whispers.

Graves

Do this and you will be honoured among wizards. For ever.

Graves pulls Credence into a hug which, with his hand on Credence's neck, seems more controlling than affectionate. Credence, overwhelmed by the seeming affection, closes his eyes and relaxes slightly.

Graves slowly backs away, stroking Credence's neck. Credence keeps his eyes closed, longing for the human contact to continue.

Graves (whispers)
The child is dying, Credence. Time is running out.

Abruptly, Graves strides back down the alleyway and Disapparates.

Scene 80

Ext. Rooftop with Pigeon Coop—Dusk

A rooftop overlooking the whole city. In the middle sits a small wooden shed, which houses a pigeon coop.

Newt steps up onto a ledge and stands looking over the immense city. Pickett sits on his shoulder, clicking.

Jacob is inside the shed, looking at the pigeon coop as Queenie enters.

Queenie
    Your grandfather kept pigeons? Mine bred owls. I used to love feeding 'em.

Angle on Newt and Tina – Tina has joined Newt in standing on the ledge.

Tina
   Graves always insisted the disturbances were caused by a beast. We
need to catch all your creatures, so he
can't keep using them as a scapegoat.

Newt
   There's only one still missing. Dougal,
my Demiguise.

Tina
   Dougal?

Newt
   Slight problem is that . . . um, he's
invisible.

Tina **(this is so ridiculous that she
can't help but smile)**
   Invisible?

Newt
   Yes – most of the time . . . he
does . . . um . . .

Tina
How do you catch something that—

Newt (beginning to smile)
With immense difficulty.

Tina
Oh ...

They smile at each other – there's a new warmth between them, Newt still awkward but somehow unable to stop staring at Tina as she smiles.

Tina moves slowly towards Newt.

A beat.

Tina
Gnarlak!

Newt (taken aback)
Excuse me?

Tina (conspiratorial, excited)
Gnarlak – he was an informant of mine when I was an Auror! He used to trade in magical creatures on the side—

Newt
He wouldn't happen to have an interest in paw prints would he?

Tina
He's interested in anything he can sell.

Scene 81

Ext. The Blind Pig— Night

Tina leads the group down an insalubrious back alley covered in bins, crates and discarded objects. She locates a set of steps leading to a basement apartment and motions them down.

The steps appear to lead to a dead end: the doorway has been bricked up. Instead, a poster of a simpering debutante in evening dress, gazing at herself in a mirror, covers the end of the walkway.

Tina and Queenie stand in front of this poster. They turn to each other and, in unison, raise their wands. As they do so, their work

clothes transform into stunning
flapper party dresses. Tina looks
up at Newt, somewhat
embarrassed by her new attire.
Queenie gazes at Jacob, a cheeky
smile on her face.

Tina steps towards the poster
and slowly raises her hand. As she
does so, the eyes of the debutante
move upwards, following her every
move. Tina knocks slowly on the
door four times.

Newt, sensing the need for a
change, hastily magics himself
a small bow tie. Jacob looks on,
jealously.

A hatch opens: the painted eyes of
the debutante whip back to reveal
the gaze of a suspicious guard.

Scene 82

Int. The Blind Pig— Night

A seedy, low-ceilinged speak-easy for the down and out of New York's magical community. Every witch and wizard criminal in New York is here, their wanted posters hanging proudly on the walls. A glimpse of 'Gellert Grindelwald: Wanted for No–Maj Slayings in Europe'.

A glamorous goblin Jazz Singer croons on a stage full of goblin musicians, smoky images wafting from her wand to illustrate her lyrics. All is dingy and shabby, an atmosphere of menacing fun.

Jazz Singer
The phoenix cried fat tears of
pearl,

When the dragon snapped up
his best girl,

And the Billywig forgot to
twirl,

When his sweetheart left him
cold,

And the unicorn done lost his
horn,

And the Hippogriff feels all
forlorn,

'Cause their lady loves have
upped and gawn,

Or that's what I've been
told—

**Jacob stands at the seemingly
unmanned bar, waiting to be served.**

Jacob
How do I get a drink in this joint?

**Out of nowhere, a thin bottle
of brown liquid zooms towards him.
He catches it, stunned.**

The head of a House–Elf peers up at him from behind the bar.

House–Elf
What? Ain't you ever seen a house-elf before?

Jacob
Oh, no, yeah, no, yeah of course I have ... I love house-elves.

Jacob tries to act nonchalant – he removes the cork from the bottle.

Jacob
My uncle's a house-elf.

The House–Elf – not fooled – raises himself up, leaning on the bar to stare at Jacob.

Queenie approaches. She looks downcast as she orders.

Queenie
Six shots of gigglewater and a lobe blaster, please.

The House-Elf reluctantly shuffles off to fulfil her request. Jacob and Queenie look at each other. Jacob reaches out and takes one of the gigglewater shots.

Queenie
Are all No-Majs like you?

Jacob **(trying to be serious, almost seductive)**
No, I'm the only one like me.

Maintaining strong eye contact with Queenie, Jacob knocks back the shot. Suddenly he emits a raucous, high-pitched giggle. Queenie laughs sweetly at his look of surprise.

Angle on a House-Elf serving a drink to a giant, whose hand dwarfs the mug he is handed.

Angle on Newt and Tina sitting at a table alone. There's an awkward silence. Newt studies the characters in the room: hooded and heavily scarred witches and wizards gamble magical artefacts in a game with runic dice.

Tina (looking around)
I've arrested half of the people in here.

Newt
You can tell me to mind my own business ... but I saw something in that death potion back there. I saw you – hugging – that Second Salem boy.

Tina
His name's Credence. His mother beats him. She beats all those kids she adopted, but she seems to hate him the most.

Newt (realising)
And she was the No-Maj you attacked?

Tina
That's how I lost my job. I went for her in front of a meeting of her crazy followers – they all had to be Obliviated. It was a big scandal.

Queenie signals from across the room.

Queenie (whispers)
It's him.

Gnarlak has emerged from the depths of the speakeasy. Smoking a cigar and smartly dressed, for a goblin, he has a sly, smooth demeanour like a mafia boss. He eyes the newcomers as he walks.

Jazz Singer **(O.S.)**
  Yes, love has set the beasts astir,

  The dang'rous and the meek concur,

  It's ruffled feathers, fleece and fur,

  'Cause love drives all of us wild.

Gnarlak sits himself at the end of their table, an air of confidence and dangerous control. A House-Elf hastily brings him a drink.

Gnarlak
  So – you're the guy with the case full of monsters, huh?

Newt
  News travels fast. I was hoping you'd be able to tell me if there have been any sightings. Tracks. That sort of thing.

Gnarlak downs his drink. Another House–Elf brings him a document to sign.

Gnarlak
You've got a big price on your head, Mr Scamander. Why should I help you instead of turnin' you in?

Newt
I take it I'll have to make it worth your while?

The House–Elf scurries off holding the signed document.

Gnarlak
Hmm – let's consider it a cover charge.

Newt pulls out a couple of Galleons and slides them across the table towards Gnarlak, who barely looks up.

Gnarlak **(not impressed)**
Huh – **Macusa**'s offerin' more'n that.

A beat.

Newt pulls out a beautiful metal instrument and places it on the table.

Gnarlak
Lunascope? I got five.

Newt rummages in his coat pocket and pulls out a glowing, frozen ruby egg instead.

Newt
Frozen Ashwinder egg!

Gnarlak **(finally interested)**
You see – now we're—

Gnarlak suddenly spots Pickett, who is peeking out of Newt's pocket.

Gnarlak
—wait a minute – that's a Bowtruckle, right?

Pickett quickly retreats and Newt puts a hand protectively over his pocket.

Newt
No.

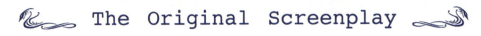

Gnarlak
　Ah, come on, that's a Bowtruckle –
they pick locks – am I right?

Newt
　You're not having him.

Gnarlak
　Well, good luck gettin' back alive,
Mr Scamander, what with the whole of
Macusa on your back.

　**Gnarlak gets up and walks
away.**

Newt **(in agony)**
　All right.

　**Gnarlak, turned away from Newt,
smiles viciously.**

　**Newt extracts Pickett from
his pocket. Pickett clings to
Newt's hands, madly clicking and
whining.**

Newt
　Pickett . . .

Newt slowly hands Pickett over to Gnarlak. Pickett reaches his little arms forward, imploring Newt to take him back. Newt cannot look at him.

Gnarlak
Ah, yeah ...

(to Newt)

Somethin' invisible's been wreakin' havoc around Fifth Avenue. You may wanna check out Macy's department store. Might help what you're looking for.

Newt **(sotto voce)**
Dougal ...

(to Gnarlak)

Right, one last thing. There's a Mr Graves who works at **Macusa** – I was wondering what you knew of his background.

Gnarlak stares. A sense that there is much that he could say – and that he'd rather die than say it.

Gnarlak
You ask too many questions, Mr
Scamander. That can get you killed.

**Angle on a House-Elf carrying
a crate of bottles.**

House-Elf
Macusa are coming!

**The House-Elf Disapparates.
Other customers throughout the bar
hurriedly do the same.**

Tina **(getting to her feet)**
You tipped them off!

**Gnarlak stares at them, chuckling
menacingly.**

**Behind Queenie, the wanted
posters on the wall update to show
Newt and Tina's faces.**

**Aurors begin Apparating into the
speakeasy.**

**Jacob, seemingly innocent,
saunters up to Gnarlak.**

Jacob
>   Sorry, Mr Gnarlak—

Jacob punches Gnarlak straight in the face, knocking him backwards. Queenie looks delighted.

Jacob
>   – reminds me of my foreman!

Throughout the bar, various customers are being apprehended by the Aurors.

Newt scrambles about on the floor looking for Pickett. Around him people are running, diving away from Aurors, trying to escape the bar. Newt finally finds Pickett on a table leg, grabs him and runs towards his group.

Jacob grabs another shot of gigglewater and knocks it back. He giggles uproariously as Newt grabs his elbow and the group Disapparates.

Scene 83

Int. Second Salem Church—Night

The long room is dimly lit by one set of lights. There's barely any noise.

Chastity sits primly at the long table in the middle of the church. She formulaically arranges leaflets and places them in little bags.

Modesty sits opposite in a night-dress, reading a book. In the deep background, Mary Lou busies herself in her bedroom.

Modesty is the only one to register a small clunk from upstairs.

Scene 84

Int. Modesty's Bedroom—Night

A bleak room. A single bed, an oil-lamp, a sampler on the wall: An Alphabet of Sin. Modesty's dolls lined up on a shelf. One with a little noose around its neck, another tied to a stake.

Credence scrabbles to get underneath Modesty's bed. He looks among the boxes and objects hidden there, then suddenly stops, staring ...

Scene 85

Int. Second Salem
Church—Night

**Modesty stands at the bottom
of the stairs, looking up.
She slowly ascends.**

Scene 86

Int. Modesty's Bedroom—Night

Angle on Credence's face under the bed – Credence has found a toy wand. He stares, unable to draw his eyes from it.

Behind him, Modesty enters.

Modesty
Whatchoo doin', Credence?

Credence bangs his head on the bed in his haste to get out. He emerges, dusty and scared. He is relieved to see that it is only Modesty but she, on seeing the wand, is terrified.

Credence
    Where'd you get this?

Modesty **(frightened whisper)**
    Give it back, Credence. It's just a toy!

The door bangs open. Mary Lou enters. Her gaze travels from Modesty to Credence and the toy wand – she is angrier than we have ever seen her.

Mary Lou **(to Credence)**
    What is this?

Scene 87

Int. Second Salem Church—Night

Hold on Chastity, still filling bags with leaflets.

Mary Lou **(O.S.)**
Take it off!

Chastity glances up towards the landing.

Scene 88

Int. Second Salem Church, Upstairs Landing—Night

Mary Lou stands on the landing overlooking the main church below. Seen from below her figure is powerful, almost deified.

Mary Lou turns back towards Credence and slowly, her face full of loathing, snaps the wand in two.

As Modesty cowers, Credence begins to remove his belt. Mary Lou holds out her hand and takes it.

Credence **(pleading)**
    Ma . . .

Mary Lou
    I am not your ma! Your mother was
a wicked, unnatural woman!

**Modesty forces her way between
them.**

Modesty
    It was mine.

Mary Lou
    Modesty—

**Suddenly the belt is whipped out
of Mary Lou's hands by supernatural
means and falls like a dead snake in
a far corner. Mary Lou looks at her
hand – it is cut and bleeding from the
force of the movement.**

**Mary Lou is stunned – she
glances between Modesty and
Credence.**

Mary Lou **(frightened but covering it)**
    What is this?

**Modesty stares defiantly directly
back at her. In the background**

we see Credence crouched down, hugging his knees and shaking.

Trying to remain composed, Mary Lou moves slowly to retrieve the belt. Before she can touch it, the belt slithers away across the floor.

Mary Lou backs away, tears of fear welling in her eyes. She turns slowly back towards the children.

As she moves, an almighty force explodes into her: a bestial, screeching, dark mass that consumes her. Her scream is blood-curdling as the force throws her backwards, striking a wooden beam, flinging her over the balcony.

Mary Lou smashes down onto the floor of the main church, her body lifeless, her face bearing the same scars seen on the face of Senator Shaw.

The Dark force flies through the church, upending the table and destroying everything in sight.

Scene 89

Ext. Department Store—Night

Wide shot of a department store, its windows full of glamorously dressed mannequins.

Jacob approaches the shop windows staring at a handbag which, seemingly of its own accord, is sliding down the arm of a mannequin. Newt, Tina and Queenie hurry up behind him and watch as the bag hovers in mid-air and floats off into the store.

Scene 90

Int. Department Store—Night

A well-presented department store decorated for Christmas, with aisles full of expensive jewellery, shoes, hats and perfume. The place is shut down for the night, all the lights are off, no noises can be heard.

We see the handbag float down the central aisle, accompanied by small grunting noises.

Newt and the group quickly tiptoe through the store, coming to hide behind a large plastic Christmas display. They eye up the floating handbag.

Newt **(whispers)**
So Demiguises are fundamentally peaceful, but they can give a nasty nip if provoked.

The Demiguise itself appears – a silvery-haired, orangutan-like creature, with a curious, wizened face – clambering over a display to reach a box of sweets.

Newt **(to Jacob and Queenie)**
You two ... head that way.

They start moving.

Newt
And try very hard not to be predict-able.

Jacob and Queenie exchange perplexed glances before heading off.

A small roar can be heard in the distance.

Angle on the Demiguise which, on hearing the sound, looks up towards the ceiling, before continuing

to gather sweets, now shovelling them into its handbag.

Tina **(O.S.)**
Was that the Demiguise?

Newt
No, I think it might be the reason that the Demiguise is here.

Angle on Newt and Tina, moving swiftly down an aisle towards the Demiguise, which is now moving away through the store.

Realising it's been spotted, the Demiguise turns and looks at Newt quizzically, before moving up a set of side stairs. Newt smiles and moves to follow.

Scene 91

Int. Department Store, Attic Storeroom—Night

A huge, dark attic-space, filled floor to ceiling with shelves packed with boxes of china: dinner services, teacups and general kitchenware.

The Demiguise walks along the attic in a patch of moonlight. It glances around before stopping and emptying its handbag full of confectionery.

Newt **(O.S.)**
    Its sight operates on probability, so it can foresee the most likely immediate future.

Newt comes into view, creeping up behind the Demiguise.

Tina **(O.S.)**
    So what's it doing now?

Newt
    It's babysitting.

The Demiguise holds up one of the sweets, seeming to offer it up to someone or something.

Tina
    What did you just say—?

Newt **(calm and whispering)**
    This is my fault. I thought I had them all – but I must have miscounted.

Jacob and Queenie enter quietly. Newt moves calmly forwards and kneels beside the Demiguise, which makes space for him in front of the sweets. Newt carefully places his case down.

Angle on Tina, a shift of light reveals the scales of a large creature

hiding in the rafters of the attic. Tina looks up in horror.

Tina
    It was babysitting that?

Angle on the ceiling as the face of an Occamy comes into view – just like the small blue snake-like birds seen in the case, this Occamy is huge, coiled round and round itself to fill the entire attic roof-space.

The Occamy moves slowly down towards Newt and the Demiguise who, again, offers up a sweet. Newt remains very still.

Newt
    Occamies are choranaptyxic. So they – grow – to fill – available – space.

The Occamy spots Newt, and cranes its head towards him. Newt holds up a hand, gently.

Newt
    Mummy's here.

Angle on the Demiguise, whose eyes flash a brilliant blue – a sign that it's having a premonition.

Flashcuts:

A Christmas bauble rolls across the floor; the Occamy is panicking, Newt clasping its back, being flung about the room; the Demiguise is suddenly on Jacob's back.

Back to the Demiguise as its eyes turn back to brown.

Queenie moves slowly forward, staring at the Occamy. As she does so she accidentally kicks a tiny glass bauble on the floor, which jingles as it rolls. At the sound, the Occamy rears up, screeching. Newt tries to calm the large creature.

Newt
  Woah! Woah!

Jacob and Queenie stagger backwards to find cover. The Demiguise runs away and jumps into Jacob's arms.

The Occamy swoops, scooping Newt up onto its back as it violently thrashes about the attic, sending shelves flying. Newt shouts out.

Newt
    Right, we need an insect, any kind of insect – and a teapot! Find a teapot!

Tina army-crawls through the chaos, dodging falling items, trying to find what Newt has asked for.

The wings of the Occamy crash down to the floor, narrowly missing Jacob as he stumbles around, encumbered by the Demiguise now clinging to his back.

Newt finds it harder and harder to hold on as the Occamy becomes more and more distressed, its wings now thrashing upwards, destroying the roof of the building.

Jacob turns, he and the Demiguise spotting a stray cockroach on a crate. Jacob reaches his hand up to grab it, when part of the Occamy crashes

down, destroying the crate and his chance.

Angle on Tina, crawling across the floor with great determination, in hot pursuit of a cockroach.

Angle on Queenie, who screams as she's knocked to the floor by the force of the Occamy. Jacob runs up behind her and dives forwards, flat onto the floor, finally laying claim to a cockroach. Tina stands, clutching a teapot and screaming.

Tina
    Teapot!

At this noise, the Occamy rears its head once more, causing its tail to writhe, squashing and pinning Jacob – with the Demiguise – against one of the rafters.

Jacob and Tina are now at opposite ends of the room, neither daring to move, swathes of Occamy scales between them.

Angle on Jacob and the Demiguise – the Demiguise looks shiftily up to the side and promptly vanishes. Jacob slowly turns to follow the Demiguise's gaze – the Occamy's face is inches away from his own, staring with full intensity at the cockroach in his hand. Jacob barely dares to breathe.

Newt peers round from behind the Occamy's head and whispers.

Newt
Roach in teapot ...

Jacob gulps, trying not to make eye contact with the huge creature next to him.

Jacob **(trying to soothe the Occamy)**
Shhhh!

Jacob widens his eyes at Tina, warning her of his intent.

In Slow Motion:

Jacob throws the roach. We watch it soar through the air as the Occamy's body begins to move once more, uncurling and swirling round the room.

Newt jumps from the Occamy's back, landing safely on the floor, while Queenie takes cover, placing a colander over her head.

Tina runs, teapot outstretched, hurdling over the Occamy's coils as she goes – a heroic sight. She lands on her knees in the centre of the room, the cockroach falling perfectly into the teapot.

The Occamy rears up, shrinking rapidly as it rises, before diving down head first. Tina lowers her head, bracing herself for a hit. The Occamy races down towards the teapot, and glides seamlessly inside.

Newt races forwards and jams a lid on top of the teapot. He and Tina breathe heavily: relief.

Newt

Choranaptyxic. They also **shrink** to fit the available space.

Angle inside the teapot – the now tiny Occamy gobbling down its cockroach.

Tina

Tell me the truth – was that everything that came out of the case?

Newt

That's everything – and that's the truth.

Scene 92

Int. Newt's Case—Shortly Afterwards—Night

Jacob holds the Demiguise's hand, leading it through its enclosure.

Newt **(O.S.)**
Here she comes.

Jacob lifts the Demiguise up and into its nest.

Jacob **(to the Demiguise)**
Happy to be home? Bet you're exhausted buddy. Come on – there you go – that's right.

Tina is tentatively holding the

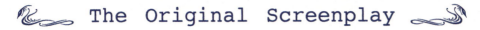

baby Occamy. Supervised by Newt, she places it gently into its nest.

Hold on Tina as she looks around at the Erumpent, now stamping through her enclosure. Tina's face is full of wonder and admiration. Jacob chuckles at her expression.

Pickett gives Newt a sharp pinch from inside his pocket.

Newt
Ouch!

Newt fishes Pickett out, holding him up on his hand as he walks through the various enclosures.

We see the Niffler sitting in a small enclave, surrounded by its various treasures.

Newt
Right ... I think we need to talk. See, I wouldn't have let him keep you, Pickett. Pick, I would rather chop off my hand than get rid of you ... after everything you have done for me – now come on.

Newt has reached Frank's area.

Newt
　　Pick – we've talked about
sulking before, haven't we? Pickett –
come on give me a smile. Pickett, give
me a ...

**Pickett sticks out his tiny tongue
and blows a raspberry at Newt.**

Newt
　　All right – now, that is beneath you.

**Newt places Pickett on his
shoulder and starts busying himself
with various buckets of feed.**

**Angle on a photograph inside
Newt's shed, which shows a beautiful
girl – the girl smiles suggestively.
Queenie stares at the photo.**

Queenie
　　Hey, Newt. Who is she?

Newt
　　Ah ... that's no one.

Queenie **(reading his mind)**
    Leta Lestrange? I've heard of that family. Aren't they kinda – you know?

Newt
    Please don't read my mind.

A beat as Queenie drinks the whole story out of Newt's head. She looks both intrigued and saddened. Newt continues to work, trying hard to pretend Queenie isn't reading his mind.

Queenie steps forwards, closer to Newt.

Newt **(angry, embarrassed)**
    Sorry, I asked you not to.

Queenie
    I know, I'm sorry, I can't help it. People are easiest to read when they're hurting.

Newt
    I'm not hurting. Anyway, it was a long time ago.

Queenie
That was a real close friendship you had at school.

Newt (attempting to be dismissive)
Yes, well, neither of us really fitted in at school, so we—

Queenie
—became real close. For years.

In the background we see Tina, who has noticed that Newt and Queenie are talking.

Queenie (concerned)
She was a taker. You need a giver.

Tina walks towards them.

Tina
What are you two talking about?

Newt
Ah nothing.

Queenie
School.

Newt
    School.

Jacob **(putting on his jacket)**
    Did you say school? Is there a school?
A wizardry school here? In America?

Queenie
    Of course – Ilvermorny! It's only the
best wizard school in the whole world!

Newt
    I think you'll find the best wizarding
school in the world is Hogwarts!

Queenie
    Hogwash.

**A gigantic crack of thunder. The
Thunderbird, Frank, rises into the air
screeching, flapping his wings vigor-
ously, his body turning black and
gold, his eyes flashing lightning.**

**Newt stands, examining the bird,
concerned.**

Newt
    Danger. He senses danger.

Scene 93

Ext. Second Salem Church—Night

Graves Apparates in the shadows. Wand drawn, he slowly approaches the church, examining the scene of decimation. Rather than nervous, he seems intrigued, almost excited.

Scene 94

Int. Second Salem Church—Night

The place is destroyed – moon-light filters through gaps in the roof, and Chastity lies dead amid debris from the attack.

Graves slowly enters the church, wand still drawn. Eerie sobbing can be heard from somewhere in the building.

Mary Lou's body lies on the floor in front of him – the marks on her face visible in the moonlight. Graves considers the corpse: a realisation dawning on his face – no horror, merely wariness and intense interest.

**Focus on Credence, cowering
at the back of the church,
whimpering and clutching his
pendant of the Deathly Hallows.
Graves steps quickly towards him,
bends down, cradling Credence's
head. However, there's little
tenderness to his voice as
he speaks.**

Graves
    The Obscurial – was here? Where did she go?

**Credence looks up into Graves's
face – he is utterly traumatised and
unable to explain – his face a plea for
affection.**

Credence
    Help me. Help me.

Graves
    Didn't you tell me you had another sister?

**Credence begins to weep again.
Graves places a hand on his neck,**

his face contorting with stress as he
tries to remain calm.

Credence
Please help me.

Graves
Where's your other sister, Credence?
The little one? Where did she go?

Credence trembles and mumbles.

Credence
Please help me.

**Suddenly vicious, Graves slaps
Credence hard across the face.**

**Credence, stunned, stares at
Graves.**

Graves
Your sister's in grave danger. We
need to find her.

**Credence is aghast, unable to
comprehend that his hero has hit him.
Graves grabs him and pulls him up
onto his feet, as they Disapparate.**

Scene 95

Ext. Tenement In The Bronx—Night

A deserted street. Graves, led by Credence, approaches a tenement building.

Scene 96

Int. Tenement In The Bronx, Hallway—Night

Inside, the building is miserable, dilapidated. Credence and Graves climb the stairwell.

Graves **(O.S.)**
  What is this place?

Credence
  Ma adopted Modesty out of here. From a family of twelve. She still misses her brothers and sisters. She still talks about them.

  Graves, wand in hand, looks around the landing – there are numerous darkened doorways stretching out in several directions.

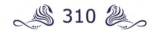

Credence, still shell-shocked, has stopped in the stairwell.

Graves
 Where is she?

Credence looks down – at a loss.

Credence
 I don't know.

Graves becomes increasingly impatient – he's so close to his goal. He marches forward into one of the rooms.

Graves **(contemptuous)**
 You're a Squib, Credence. I could smell it off you the minute I met you.

Credence's face falls.

Credence
 What?

Graves marches back along the corridor to try another room. His pretence of care for Credence all but forgotten.

Graves
> You have magical ancestry, but no power.

Credence
> But you said you could teach me—

Graves
> You're unteachable. Your mother's dead. That's your reward.

Graves points to another landing.

Graves
> I'm done with you.

Credence doesn't move. He stares after Graves, his breathing becoming shallow and quick, as though he's trying to contain something.

Graves moves through the dark rooms. A tiny movement somewhere close.

Graves
> Modesty?

Graves advances cautiously into a derelict schoolroom at the end of a corridor.

Scene 97

Int. Tenement In The Bronx, Derelict Room— Night

Angle on Modesty cowering in a corner, wide-eyed with fear and shaking as Graves approaches.

Graves **(whispering)**
Modesty.

Graves bends down and puts his wand away – once again playing the soothing parent.

Graves **(gentle)**
There's no need to be afraid.

I'm here with your brother, Credence.

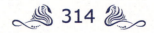

Modesty whimpers with terror at the mention of Credence.

Graves
    Out you come now ...

Graves extends his hand.

A faint jingle sounds.

Angle on the ceiling as cracks begin to appear, spreading like a spider's web. Dust begins to fall as the walls shake uncontrollably, the room beginning to disintegrate around them.

Graves stands. He looks down at Modesty, but she is clearly terrified and not the source of this magic. Graves turns and slowly draws his wand, the wall in front of him collapsing as though turned to sand, revealing another wall ahead. Modesty is nothing to him now.

As each wall collapses in front of him he is transfixed, elated, yet also aware that he has made a colossal error ...

The final wall collapses. He is facing Credence, who stares at him, unable to control his fury, his sense of betrayal, his bitterness.

Graves
　　Credence ... I owe you an apology ...

Credence
　　I trusted you. I thought you were my friend. That you were different.

Credence's face begins to contort, his rage tearing him from within.

Graves
　　You can control it, Credence.

Credence **(whispers, making eye contact finally)**
　　But I don't think I want to, Mr Graves.

The Obscurus moves horribly beneath Credence's skin. An awful inhuman growl comes out of his mouth, from which something dark begins to bloom.

This force finally takes over Credence, his whole body exploding into a dark mass which hurtles forwards out of the window, narrowly missing Graves.

Graves stands, watching as the Obscurus zooms out and over the city.

Scene 98

Ext. Tenement In The Bronx—Night

We follow the Obscurus as it churns and twists through the city, wreaking havoc: cars are sent flying, pavements explode and buildings are demolished – the Obscurus leaves only destruction in its wake.

Scene 99

Ext. Squire's Rooftop—Night

Newt, Tina, Jacob and Queenie stand on the rooftop underneath a large 'Squire's' sign. From the edge they have a clear view of the chaos going on below.

Jacob **(overstimulated)**
Jeez ... is that the Obscuria-thing?

Sirens sound. Newt is staring, registering the scale of the destruction.

Newt
That's more powerful than any Obscurial I have ever heard of ...

A particularly loud explosion in the distance. The city beneath them is starting to burn. Newt thrusts his case into Tina's hands and takes a journal from his pocket.

Newt
　　If I don't come back, look after my creatures. Everything that you need to know is in there.

He hands her the journal, barely able to make eye contact.

Tina
　　What?

Newt **(looking back to the Obscurus)**
　　They're not killing it.

Their eyes meet – a moment full of what they might have said to each other – before Newt jumps from the roof and Disapparates.

Tina **(distraught)**
　　Newt!

Tina slams the case into Queenie's arms.

Tina
> You heard him – look after them!

Tina also Disapparates. Queenie shoves the case at Jacob.

Queenie
> Keep holda that, honey.

She moves to Disapparate, but Jacob hangs on to her and she falters.

Jacob
> No, no, no!

Queenie
> I can't take you. Please let go of me, Jacob!

Jacob
> Hey, hey! You're the one that said I was one of youse ... right?

Queenie
> It's too dangerous.

A further massive explosion in the distance. Jacob tightens his grip on Queenie. She reads his mind and her expression changes to one of wonderment and tenderness as she sees what he went through in the war. Queenie is moved and appalled. Very slowly, she raises a hand and touches his cheek.

Scene 100

Ext. Times Square— Night

The scene is one of total chaos. Buildings are on fire, people scream and run in all directions, cars lie destroyed in the road.

Graves prowls through the Square, oblivious to the distress around him, his focus concentrated on only one thing.

The Obscurus writhes at one end of the Square, its energy angrier now – moving through layers of hurt and anguish, the products of isolation and torment – flecks of red light roaring from within. Credence's face is just discernible within the mass, distorted, pained.

 325

Graves stands before it, triumphant.

Newt Apparates from further down the street and watches.

Graves **(shouting to reach Credence over the almighty noise)**
To survive so long, with this inside you Credence, is a miracle. You are a miracle. Come with me – think of what we could achieve together.

The Obscurus moves closer to Graves – we hear a scream from within the mass as its Dark energy bursts out once more, knocking Graves to the ground. The force sends a shockwave round the Square – Newt dives behind a fallen car for cover.

Tina Apparates into the Square and takes cover by another burning vehicle close to Newt. They look at each other.

Tina
Newt!

Newt

It's the Second Salem boy. He's the Obscurial.

Tina

He's not a child.

Newt

I know – but I saw him – his power must be so strong – he's somehow managed to survive. It's incredible.

As the Obscurus screams once more, Tina makes a decision.

Tina

Newt! Save him.

Tina dashes out towards Graves. Newt, understanding, Disapparates.

Scene 101

Ext. Times Square—Night

Graves is moving nearer and nearer to the Obscurus, which continues to scream and wail at his presence. He takes out his wand, poised ...

Tina runs into view behind Graves. She fires at him, but he turns just in time – his reactions marvellous, astounding.

The Obscurus now vanishes. Graves, thoroughly irritated, advances on Tina, deflecting her spells with perfect ease.

Graves
    Tina. You're always turning up where you are least wanted.

Graves summons an abandoned car, which whooshes through the air, forcing Tina to dive out of the way, just in time.

By the time Tina has gathered herself up from the ground, Graves has Disapparated.

Scene 102

Int. Major Investigation Department, Macusa—Night

A metallic map of New York City lights up to show areas of intense magical activity. Madam Picquery, surrounded by top Aurors, looks on, aghast.

Madam Picquery
    Contain this, or we are exposed and it will mean war.

The Aurors immediately Disapparate.

Scene 103

Ext. Rooftops of New York—Night

Newt race–Apparates as fast as he can across the tops of buildings in pursuit of the Obscurus.

Newt
   Credence! Credence! I can help you.

The Obscurus dives towards Newt, who Disapparates just in time, before continuing to chase it across the rooftops.

As he runs, spells explode around him, disintegrating the rooftops. A dozen Aurors have appeared, attacking the Obscurus from ahead, and almost taking out Newt, who

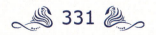

leaps for cover, trying desperately to keep up.

The Obscurus veers to avoid the spells, leaving black snow-like parti-cles that drift across the rooftops as it retreats screaming, and turns down another block.

In a particularly vigorous display, the Obscurus now rises dramatically up into the air, as spells in electric blue and white hit it from all angles. Finally it crashes to the ground and races along a wide, empty street – a black tsunami destroying anything in its path.

Scene 104

Ext. Outside a Subway Station—Night

A line of policemen stand with their guns aimed at the terri-fying supernatural force powering towards them.

Their faces turn from confused alarm to total panic as they see the mass swarming ahead, making straight for them. They fire their guns – their efforts futile in the face of such a seemingly unstoppable kinetic mass. Finally they disband, fleeing down the street, just as the Obscurus reaches them.

Scene 105

Ext. Rooftops/Streets of New York—Night

Angle on Newt, standing on top of a skyscraper looking out as the Obscurus rises up over the surrounding buildings and slams spectacularly into the ground just outside the City Hall subway entrance.

Sudden quiet. A pulsing, heaving, screechy breathing emanates from the Obscurus where it rests at the entrance.

Finally, as Newt watches, we see the black mass shrink to nothing, and the small figure of Credence descends the steps into the subway.

 334

Scene 106

Int. Subway—Night

Newt Apparates into the City Hall subway, a long, mosaiced Art Deco station tunnel, which bears the signs of having been crossed by the Obscurus: the chandelier creaks, a few tiles have fallen. We can hear its deep breathing, cornered, like a frightened panther.

Newt creeps along the platform, trying to find the epicentre of the sound, as the Obscurus slides down the ceiling.

Scene 107

Ext. Subway Entrance— Night

Aurors surround the entrance to the subway. Pointing their wands at the pavement and into the sky, they draw an invisible energy field around the entrance.

We hear more Aurors arrive, among them Graves – scanning, calculating and immediately taking charge.

Graves
    Bar the area. I don't want anyone else down there!

As the magical field is almost complete, a figure rolls underneath it and dashes unseen into the subway – Tina.

Scene 108

Int. Subway—Night

Newt has reached the Obscurus in the shadows of a tunnel. Now much calmer, it gently swirls in the air above the train tracks. Newt hides behind a pillar as he talks.

Newt
Credence ... it's Credence isn't it? I'm here to help you, Credence. I'm not here to hurt you.

In the distance we hear footsteps, the pacing controlled, deliberate.

Newt moves out from behind the pillar, and steps onto the train tracks. Within the mass of the Obscurus we

can see a shadow of Credence, curled up, scared.

Newt
    I've met someone just like you, Credence. A girl – a young girl who'd been imprisoned, she had been locked away and she'd been punished for her magic.

Credence is listening – he never dreamed there was another. Slowly the Obscurus melts away, leaving only Credence, huddled on the train tracks – a frightened child.

Newt crouches on the floor. Credence looks to him, the tiniest trace of hope dawning in his expression: might there be a way back?

Newt
    Credence, can I come over to you? Can I come over?

Newt slowly moves forwards, but as he does so a sharp burst of light blazes out from the darkness

and a spell strikes, throwing him backwards.

Graves marches down the tunnel with intense purpose.

Credence begins to run as Graves fires further spells at Newt, who rolls out of the way towards the tunnel's central pillars. From here Newt tries to fire back, but his efforts are easily deflected.

Credence continues to lumber down the tracks but stops – a rabbit caught in the headlights – as a train approaches, its lights glaring from the darkness.

It is up to Graves to save Credence – magically casting him out of the train's path.

Scene 109

Ext. Subway Entrance— Night

Madam Picquery surveys the situation from under the magical forcefield.

Angle from the crowd and police's POV:

People begin to swarm around the subway, their cries and chatter becoming louder as they stare at the magical bubble surrounding the subway. Reporters have appeared, photographing the scene with an increased frenzy.

Shaw Sr and Barker push their way through the crowd.

Shaw Sr

That thing killed my son – I want justice!

Close on Madam Picquery as she looks out to the crowd.

Shaw Sr **(O.S.)**

I'll expose you for who you are and what you've done.

Scene 110

Int. Subway— Night

Graves stands on the platform, continuing to duel with Newt, who stands on the train tracks. Credence cowers behind Newt.

Finally, almost bored by Newt's efforts, Graves casts a spell that ripples along the train tracks and down the tunnel, finally blasting into Newt, throwing him high into the air.

Newt lands on his back and Graves immediately sets upon him, casting spells in a whip-like motion with increasing vigour. Graves's immense power is

evident, as Newt writhes on the ground, unable to stop him.

Scene 111

Ext. Subway Entrance— Night

Wide shot:

We see the luminous wall of vibrating energy now flashing with the power of the magic it contains.

Langdon, drunk, stares, enthralled and amazed by the spectacle.

Shaw Sr (to the photographers around him)
Look! Take photos!

Scene 112

Int. Subway—Night

Graves continues to whip Newt, a manic, crazed look in his eyes.

Close on Credence, further down the tunnel, sobbing. He begins to shake, his face slowly turning black as he tries to stop the kinetic mass from rising up within him.

As Newt cries out in pain, Credence succumbs to the blackness – his body enveloped and overcome – the Obscurus rising up and blasting down the tunnel towards Graves.

Graves is mesmerised – he falls to his knees beneath the vast black mass – pleading in wonder.

Graves
  Credence.

The Obscurus lets out an unearthly scream and dives towards Graves, who Disapparates just in time. The Obscurus continues to blast around the tunnel.

Graves and Newt Disapparate and Apparate around the subway trying to avoid the Obscurus's path. This causes the station to disintegrate even faster. Suddenly, the force accelerates, becoming a giant wave that consumes the entire space before flying out through the roof.

Scene 113

Ext. Subway Entrance– Night

The Obscurus crashes up through the pavement, watched by wizards and No-Majs alike. It storms up a half-built skyscraper, windows shattering at every level, electric wiring exploding, until it reaches the skeletal framework of scaffolding above, which buckles perilously.

Below it, the crowd outside the magical cordon runs for cover, terrified.

The Obscurus forms a wide disc shape before plunging back down into the subway.

Scene 114

Int. Subway—Night

The Obscurus screams and dives, bursting through the subway roof – for a split second, both Newt and Graves seem on the point of death as they lie on the tracks, cowering beneath this Dark force.

Tina **(O.S.)**
   Credence, no!

Tina runs onto the tracks.

Inches from Graves's face, the Obscurus freezes. Slowly, very slowly, it rises back up, swirling more gently, staring at Tina, who looks straight back into its weird eyes.

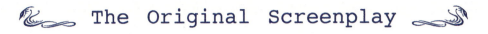

Tina
    Don't do this – please.

Newt
    Keep talking, Tina. Keep talking to
him – he'll listen to you. He's listening.

**Inside the Obscurus, Credence
reaches out to Tina, the only person
who has ever done him an uncom-
plicated kindness. He looks at her,
desperate and afraid. He has dreamed
of her ever since she saved him from
a beating.**

Tina
    I know what that woman did to
you ... I know that you've suffered ...
you need to stop this now ... Newt and
I will protect you ...

Graves is on his feet.

Tina **(pointing to Graves)**
    This man – he is using you.

Graves
    Don't listen to her, Credence. I want
you to be free. It's all right.

Tina (to Credence, calming him)
That's it ...

The Obscurus is beginning to shrink. Its dreadful face is becoming more human, more like Credence's own.

Suddenly Aurors begin pouring down the steps of the subway and into the tunnel. More Aurors advance from behind Tina, their wands raised aggressively.

Tina
Shhhh! Don't, you'll frighten him.

The Obscurus lets out a terrible moan and begins to swell again. The station is crumbling. Newt and Tina wheel around, arms akimbo, both trying to protect Credence.

Graves spins to face the Aurors, wand at the ready.

Graves
Wands down! Anyone harms him – they'll answer to me—

(turning back to Credence)

Credence!

Tina
Credence ...

**The Aurors begin pelting the
Obscurus with spells.**

Graves
No!

**We see Credence from within
the black mass, his face contorted,
screaming. The tirade of spells
continues and Credence howls
in pain.**

Scene 115

Ext. Subway Entrance— Night

The magical force field surrounding the subway breaks down as people continue to flee the scene. Only Shaw Sr and Langdon stand steadfast.

Scene 116

Int. Subway—Night

Aurors continue to aim spells at the Obscurus, their efforts unrelenting and brutal.

Under this pressure, the Obscurus finally seems to implode – a white ball of magical light taking over from the black mass.

The force of the change sends Tina, Newt and the Aurors stumbling backwards.

All power subsides. Only small tatters of black matter are left – floating through the air like feathers.

Newt gets to his feet, his face racked with deep-felt grief. Tina remains on the floor, crying.

Graves, however, climbs up, back onto the platform, as close as possible to the remnants of the black mass.

The Aurors advance towards Graves.

Graves
   You fools. Do you realise what you've done?

Graves seethes as the others watch him with interest. Madam Picquery emerges from behind the Aurors, her tone steely, questioning.

Madam Picquery
   The Obscurial was killed on my orders, Mr Graves.

Graves
   Yes. And history will surely note that, Madam President.

Graves moves towards her along the platform, his tone threatening.

Graves
What was done here tonight was not right!

Madam Picquery
He was responsible for the death of a No-Maj. He risked the exposure of our community. He has broken one of our most sacred laws.

Graves **(laughing bitterly)**
A law that has us scuttling like rats in the gutter! A law that demands that we conceal our true nature! A law that directs those under its dominion to cower in fear lest we risk discovery! I ask you Madam President—

(eyes flashing to all present)

—I ask all of you. Who does this law protect? Us?

(gesturing vaguely to the No-Majs above)

Or them?

(smiling bitterly)

I refuse to bow down any longer.

**Graves walks away from the
Aurors.**

Madam Picquery **(to the Aurors
flanking her)**
Aurors, I'd like you to relieve
Mr Graves of his wand and escort him
back to—

**As Graves moves down the plat-
form a wall of white light suddenly
appears in front of him, blocking his
path.**

**Graves thinks for a moment –
a sneer of derision and irritation
crossing his face. He turns.**

**Graves strides confidently back
along the platform, firing spells at
both groups of Aurors facing him.
Spells fly back at him from all angles,
but Graves parries them all. Several**

Aurors are sent flying – Graves appears to be winning ...

In a split-second Newt pulls the cocoon from his pocket and releases it at Graves. The Swooping Evil soars around him, shielding Newt and the Aurors from Graves's spells, and giving Newt time to raise his wand.

With a sense that he's been holding this one back, he slashes it through the air: out flies a crackling rope of supernatural light that wraps itself around Graves like a whip. Graves tries to hold it off as it tightens but staggers, struggles and falls to his knees, dropping his wand.

Tina
  Accio.

Graves's wand flies into Tina's hand. Graves looks around at them, a deep hatred in his eyes.

Newt and Tina slowly advance, Newt raising his wand.

Newt
> **Revelio.**

Graves transforms. He is no longer dark, but blond and blue-eyed. He is the man on the posters. A murmur spreads through the crowd: Grindelwald.

Madam Picquery moves towards him.

Grindelwald **(with contempt)**
> Do you think **you** can hold **me**?

Madam Picquery
> We'll do our best, Mr Grindelwald.

Grindelwald stares intently at Madam Picquery, his expression of disgust turning into a small, derisory smile. He is forced to his feet by two Aurors, who move him towards the entrance.

As Grindelwald reaches Newt, he pauses – both smiling and sneering.

Grindelwald
Will we die, just a little?

He is led away up and out of the subway. Newt watches, bemused.

Time Cut:

Queenie and Jacob push their way through to the front of the Aurors. Jacob holds Newt's case.

Queenie hugs Tina. Newt stares at Jacob.

Jacob
Hey ... I figured somebody oughta keep an eye on this thing.

He hands Newt his case.

Newt **(humble, completely grateful)**
Thank you.

Madam Picquery addresses the group as she stares through the broken roof of the subway station, into the world outside.

Madam Picquery
    We owe you an apology,
Mr Scamander. But the magical
community is exposed! We cannot
Obliviate an entire city.

A beat as this sinks in.

As Newt follows Madam Picquery's gaze, he sees a tendril of black matter, a small part of the Obscurus, floating down through the roof. Unnoticed by anyone else, it eventually floats up and away, trying to reconnect with its host.

A pause. Newt's attention snaps back to the problem at hand.

Newt
    Actually, I think we can.

Time Cut:

Newt has placed his case wide open underneath the huge hole in the subway roof.

Push in close on Newt's open case.

Suddenly Frank bursts forth in a flurry of feathers and gushes of wind – the crowd of Aurors backs away. The creature is beautiful, mesmerising but scary as he flaps his powerful wings and hovers above them.

Newt moves forward – he examines Frank, a look of real tenderness and pride on his face.

Newt
I was intending to wait until we got to Arizona, but it seems like now you are our only hope, Frank.

A look between them – an understanding. Newt reaches out his arm and Frank presses his beak lovingly into the embrace – they nuzzle each other affectionately.

The assembled group watches in awe.

Newt
>I'll miss you, too.

Newt steps back, taking the flask of Swooping Evil venom from his pocket.

Newt **(to Frank)**
>You know what you've got to do.

Newt throws the vial high up into the air – Frank lets out a sharp cry, catching it in his beak and immediately soaring out of the subway.

Scene 117

Ext. New York—Sky— Dawn

No-Majs and Aurors alike shriek and recoil as Frank bursts forth from the subway, gliding into the dawn-lit sky.

We follow Frank as he rises higher and higher into the air. As his wings flap harder, faster, storm clouds congregate. Lightning flashes. We spiral upwards as Frank twists and turns, leaving New York lying far below.

Close on Frank's beak, the vial clutched tightly and finally crushed. The powerful venom spreads through the thick rain, enchanting

it, thickening it. The darkening
sky flashes a brilliant blue
and rain begins to fall.

Scene 118

Ext. Subway Entrance— Dawn

High Angle pushing down towards the crowd as they look up to the sky. As the rain falls and hits them, people move on, docile – their bad memories washed away. Each person goes about their daily business as though nothing unusual has happened.

Aurors move through the streets, performing repairing charms to rebuild the city: buildings and cars are reconstructed and streets are returned to normal.

Angle on Langdon, standing in the rain, his expression softening,

 367

growing blank as the water
runs over his face.

Angle on police looking at their
guns, confused – why do they
have them drawn? They slowly
gather themselves, putting their
weapons away.

Inside a small family home, a
young mother looks on fondly
at her family. As she takes a sip
of water, her expression
becomes blank.

Groups of Aurors continue to repair
the streets, swiftly reassembling
broken tram tracks, all traces of
destruction finally disappearing.
One Auror, passing a newsstand,
enchants the papers, removing
Newt and Tina's mugshots and
replacing them with banal
headlines about the weather.

Mr Bingley, the bank manager,
stands in his bathroom taking a
shower. As the water trickles over
him, he too is Obliviated. We see

Bingley's wife, brushing
her teeth, her expression vacant,
carefree.

Frank continues to soar through
the streets of New York, churning
up more and more rain as he goes,
his feathers shimmering a brilliant gold. Finally he glides into the
breaking New York dawn,
a magnificent sight.

Scene 119

Int. Subway Platform—Dawn

As Madam Picquery looks on, the roof of the subway is swiftly repaired.

Newt addresses the group.

Newt
    They won't remember anything. That venom has incredibly powerful Obliviative properties.

Madam Picquery **(impressed)**
    We owe you a great debt, Mr Scamander. Now – get that case out of New York.

Newt
    Yes, Madam President.

Madam Picquery begins to walk away, her pack of Aurors moving with her. Suddenly she turns back. Queenie, having read her mind, stands protectively in front of Jacob, trying to hide him.

Madam Picquery
    Is that No-Maj still here?

(on seeing Jacob)

    Obliviate him. There can be no exceptions.

Madam Picquery reads the anguish in their faces.

Madam Picquery
    I'm sorry – but even one witness ... you know the law.

A pause. She is uncomfortable at their distress.

Madam Picquery
I'll let you say goodbye.

She leaves.

Scene 120

Ext. Subway—Dawn

Jacob leads the others up the steps of the subway, Queenie following close behind him.

Rain is still falling heavily, the streets now almost empty but for a few hard-working Aurors.

Jacob has reached the top of the steps and stands, gazing into the rain. Queenie reaches out and grabs his coat, willing him not to move out into the street. Jacob turns to her.

Jacob
Hey. Hey this is for the best.

 373

(off their looks)

Yeah – I was – I was never even supposed to be here.

Jacob fights back tears. Queenie gazes up at him, her beautiful face full of distress. Tina and Newt, too, look incredibly sad.

Jacob
I was never supposed to know any of this. Everybody knows Newt only kept me around because – hey – Newt, why did you keep me around?

Newt has to be explicit. It doesn't come easily.

Newt
Because I like you. Because you're my friend and I'll never forget how you helped me, Jacob.

A beat. Jacob is overcome with emotion at Newt's answer.

Jacob
Oh!

Queenie moves forwards up the stairs towards Jacob – they stand close.

Queenie **(trying to cheer him up)**
I'll come with you. We'll go some-where – we'll go anywhere – see I ain't never gonna find anyone like—

Jacob **(bravely)**
There's loads like me.

Queenie
No ... no ... there's only one like you.

The pain is almost unbearable.

Jacob **(a beat)**
I gotta go.

Jacob turns to face the rain, and wipes his eyes.

Newt **(starting after him)**
Jacob!

Jacob **(trying to smile)**
It's okay ... it's okay ... it's okay. It's just like waking up, right?

The group smiles back at him, encouraging, trying to soothe the situation.

Looking at their faces as he moves, Jacob walks backwards into the rain. Turning his face to the sky, arms out, he allows the water to wash over him completely.

Queenie creates a magical umbrella with her wand and steps out towards Jacob. She moves in closely, tenderly stroking Jacob's face before closing her eyes and bending in to gently kiss him.

Finally she pulls slowly away, her gaze not leaving Jacob's face even for a second. Then, suddenly, she's gone, leaving Jacob standing, arms out, longingly embracing no one.

Close on Jacob's face as he fully 'wakes up', blank-faced and confused by his location and the torrential downpour he's standing in. He finally moves off through the streets – a lonely figure.

Scene 121

Ext. Jacob's Canning Factory—a Week Later— Early Evening

An exhausted Jacob, surrounded by a crowd of similarly overalled production-line workers, is leaving after a hard day's shift. He carries a battered leather case.

A man walks towards him – Newt. They collide and Jacob's case is knocked to the ground.

Newt
    So sorry – sorry!

Newt has moved swiftly and purposefully onwards.

Jacob **(no recognition)**
Hey!

Jacob bends to pick up his case and looks down, puzzled. His old case is suddenly very heavy. One of the catches flicks open of its own accord. Jacob smiles a little, and bends down to open the case.

Inside, the case is filled with solid silver Occamy eggshells, a note attached. As Jacob reads, we hear:

Newt **(V.O.)**
'Dear Mr Kowalski, You are wasted in a canning factory. Please take these Occamy eggshells as collateral for your bakery. A well-wisher.'

Scene 122

Ext. New York Harbour—Next Day

Close on Newt's feet as he walks through the crowd.

Newt is preparing to leave New York, overcoat on, Hufflepuff scarf around his neck, case tied up tightly with string.

Tina walks alongside him. They stop before the boarding gate. Tina looks anxious.

Newt **(smiling)**
Well it's been ...

Tina
Hasn't it!

 383

Pause. Newt looks up, Tina's expression is expectant.

Tina
   Listen, Newt, I wanted to thank you.

Newt
   What on earth for?

Tina
   Well, you know, if you hadn't said all those nice things to Madam Picquery about me – I wouldn't be back on the investigative team now.

Newt
   Well – I can't think of anyone that I'd rather have investigating me.

Not precisely what he was aiming for, but too late now ... Newt becomes slightly awkward, Tina shyly appreciative.

Tina
   Well try not to need investigating for a bit.

Newt
    I will. Quiet life for me from now
on ... back to the Ministry ... deliver
my manuscript ...

Tina
    I'll look out for it. **Fantastic Beasts
and Where to Find Them**.

    **Weak smiles. A pause. Tina plucks
up courage.**

Tina
    Does Leta Lestrange like to read?

Newt
    Who?

Tina
    The girl whose picture you carry—

Newt
    I don't really know what Leta
likes these days because people
change.

Tina
    Yes.

Newt (a dawning realisation)
I've changed. I think. Maybe a little.

Tina is delighted, but doesn't know how to express it. Instead, she's trying not to cry. The ship's siren sounds – most of the other passengers have now boarded.

Newt
I'll send you a copy of my book, if I may.

Tina
I'd like that.

Newt gazes at Tina – awkwardly affectionate. He gently reaches forward and touches her hair. Lingering for a moment, they stare into each other's eyes.

A last look and Newt suddenly moves away, leaving Tina standing, raising a hand to touch where Newt stroked her hair.

But then he's back.

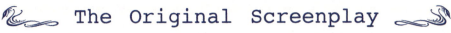
Newt
  I'm so sorry – how would you feel if
I gave you your copy in person?

**A radiant smile breaks across
Tina's face.**

Tina
  I'd like that – very much.

**Newt can't help but grin back at
her before turning and walking away.**

**He pauses on the gangplank,
perhaps unsure of how to act, but
eventually moves on without looking
back.**

**Tina stands alone in the empty
harbour. As she walks away, there's a
playful skip to her step.**

Scene 123

Ext. Jacob's Bakery, Lower East Side—Three Months Later—Day

Wide shot of a bustling New York street – market stalls line the street, which heaves with busy people, horses and carriages.

Angle on a small, inviting bakery. Crowds throng outside the pretty little shop, painted with the name 'Kowalski'. People peer with interest into the shop's windows, and happy customers leave, their arms laden with baked goods.

Scene 124

Int. Jacob's Bakery, Lower East Side—Day

Close on the doorbell as it rings to signal the entrance of a new customer.

Close on the pastries and breads on the counter, all moulded into fanciful little shapes – we recognise the Demiguise, Niffler and Erumpent among them.

Jacob, serving, is very happy, his shop full to bursting with customers.

Female Customer **(examining the little pastries)**
Where do you get your ideas from, Mr Kowalski?

Jacob
    I don't know, I don't know – they
just come!

He hands the lady her pastries.

Jacob
    Here you go – don't forget this –
enjoy.

**Jacob turns and calls over one of
his bakery assistants, handing him a
pair of keys.**

Jacob
    Hey, Henry – storage, all right?
Thanks, pal.

The bell tinkles again.

**Jacob looks up and is thunder-
struck all over again: it's Queenie.
They stare at each other – Queenie
beams, radiant. Jacob, quizzical and
totally enchanted, touches his neck –
a flicker of memory. He smiles back.**

The End

Acknowledgements

Without the patience and wisdom
of Steve Kloves and David Yates,
there would be no Fantastic Beasts
screenplay. They have my boundless
gratitude for every note, every piece
of encouragement, every improvement
they suggested. Learning, in Steve's
immortal words, to 'fit the woman to
the dress' has been a fascinating,
challenging, exasperating, exhilarating,
infuriating and ultimately rewarding
experience that I wouldn't have missed
for the world. I couldn't have done it
without them.

David Heyman has been with me from
the very first step of Harry Potter's
transition to the big screen, and
Fantastic Beasts would have been
immeasurably poorer without him. It's
been a very long journey since that
first queasy lunch in Soho, and he is
currently bringing to Newt all the

knowledge, dedication and expertise that he brought to Harry Potter.

There would be never have been a Fantastic Beasts franchise without Kevin Tsujihara. Even though I've been carrying the germ of the idea for Fantastic Beasts since 2001, when I wrote the initial book for charity, it took Kevin to make me commit to bringing Newt's story to the big screen. His support has been invaluable and he deserves the lion's share of the credit for making this happen.

Last, but never least, my family have been enormously supportive of this project even though it has meant me working through a year's worth of vacations. I don't know where I'd be without you, except that it would be a dark and lonely place where I wouldn't feel like inventing anything. So, to Neil, Jessica, David and Kenzie: thank you for being completely wonderful, funny and loving, and for still believing that I should pursue Fantastic Beasts, however tricky and time-consuming they may sometimes be.

Glossary of Film Terms

Back to scene:
After focusing on one character or action within a scene, the camera returns to the larger scene.

Close on:
The camera films a person or object from close range.

Ext.:
Exterior; an outside location.

Flashcut:
An extremely brief transition shot, sometimes as short as one frame.

High wide:
The camera is placed above, 'looking down' on the subject or scene from a wide angle.

Hold on:

The camera rests on a person or object.

Int.:

Interior; an indoor location.

Jump cut:

Cutting from one important moment to the next from the same angle. This transition is usually used to show a very brief time lapse.

Montage:

A series of shots in a sequence condensing space, time and information, often with music accompanying it.

O.S.:

Off-screen; action that takes place off-screen or dialogue that is spoken without the character being shown on screen.

Pan/whip pan:

Camera movement involving the camera turning on a stationary axis moving slowly from one subject to another; whip pan is a very fast move from one subject to the other.

POV:
Point-of-view; the camera films from a particular character's point of view.

Sotto voce:
Spoken at a whisper or under one's breath.

Time cut:
Cutting to later in the same scene.

V.O.:
Voice-over; dialogue spoken by a character not present in the scene on screen.

Wide shot:
The camera shows the entire object or human figure, usually to place it in relation to its surroundings. It is often used to set the scene in a film.

Cast and Crew

Warner Bros. Pictures Presents

a Heyday Films Production

a David Yates Film

Fantastic Beasts and Where to Find Them

Directed by	David Yates
Written by	J.K. Rowling
Produced by	David Heyman p.g.a., J.K. Rowling p.g.a., Steve Kloves p.g.a., Lionel Wigram p.g.a.
Executive Producers	Tim Lewis, Neil Blair, Rick Senat
Director of Photography	Philippe Rousselot, A.F.C./ASC
Production Designer	Stuart Craig

Editor	Mark Day
Costume Designer	Colleen Atwood
Music	James Newton Howard

Starring

Newt Scamander	Eddie Redmayne
Tina Goldstein	Katherine Waterston
Jacob Kowalski	Dan Fogler
Queenie Goldstein	Alison Sudol
Credence Barebone	Ezra Miller
Mary Lou Barebone	Samantha Morton
Henry Shaw Sr	Jon Voight
Seraphina Picquery	Carmen Ejogo
Percival Graves	Colin Farrell

About the Author

J.K. Rowling is the author of the best-selling Harry Potter series of seven books, published between 1997 and 2007, which have sold over 450 million copies worldwide, are distributed in more than 200 territories and translated into 79 languages, and have been turned into eight blockbuster films by Warner Bros. She has written three companion volumes to the series in aid of charity: **Quidditch Through the Ages** and **Fantastic Beasts and Where to Find Them** in aid of Comic Relief; and **The Tales of Beedle the Bard** in aid of her children's charity, Lumos. Her website and e-publisher Pottermore is the digital hub of the Wizarding World. She collaborated with writer Jack Thorne and director John Tiffany on the stage play **Harry Potter and the Cursed Child Parts One and Two**, which premiered in 2016 in London's West End. J.K. Rowling is also the author of a novel for adult readers, **The Casual Vacancy**, and, under the pseudonym Robert Galbraith, of three crime novels featuring private detective Cormoran Strike, which are to be adapted for BBC television. **Fantastic Beasts and Where to Find Them** is J.K. Rowling's first screenplay.

About the Book Design

The cover and illustrations in this book were based on creatures in the story and inspired by 1920s decorative style. They were drawn by hand and finished digitally in Adobe Illustrator.

The text was set in Verdana and the display type was set in Courier.